Pepsi
FIELD GUIDE

Bob Stoddard

Values and Identification

©2006 by Bob Stoddard

Published by

krause publications
An Imprint of F+W Publications

700 East State Street • Iola, WI 54990-0001
715-445-2214 • 888-457-2873

Library of Congress Catalog Number: 2006922405

ISBN 13-digit: 978-0-89689-406-8
ISBN 10-digit: 0-89689-406-1

Designed by Stacy Bloch
Edited by Dennis Thornton

Printed in China

Contents

Acknowledgments 4

About The Author 5

About Pepsi Collecting 6

Condition and Grading. 8

Reference Guide 10

A Brief History of the Pepsi-Cola® Company 12

Trademarks 21

Pepsi-Cola Advertising Slogans 28

Signs. 30

Containers. 174

Novelties, Toys, and Accessories. 262

Paper 438

Index 511

Acknowledgments

This book was made possible with the help of many friends and fellow collectors to whom I give my deepest thanks.

Collections Photographed

Lewis and Chris Carr
Scott and Kim Kinzie
John and Sara Minges
Sterling and Margaret Mann
Craig and Lisa Murray
Rick and Pam Russell
Clifford Rufkahr
Joe and Ann Donofrio
Harold Rosentreter
Dan and Judy Durbin
Dave Ezell and Maggi Pratt
Mark and Ellen Zobrist
Pepsi-Cola Bottling Company of New Haven, Missouri
Gary Metz, Muddy River Trading Company
Steve Rosentreter

Other Contributions

Michael Noll

Editors

Bob Stoddard
Sue Gustin

About The Author

Bob Stoddard is recognized as the leading authority on Pepsi-Cola memorabilia. His interest in collecting first began in 1977 with the purchase of a vintage Pepsi cooler to house an ample supply of Pepsi-Cola. As any true collector can attest, one of anything is never enough. Nearly 30 years later, his collection is one of the largest in the world, consisting of more than 3,000 items, including a rare 1909 straw holder valued over $7,000.

In 1983 Stoddard founded the Pepsi-Cola Collectors Club as a way to bring fellow collectors together to exchange information about their collections, and to buy, sell, and trade. Today, the club boasts more than 4,000 members worldwide. In exchanging information with other collectors, it became apparent to Stoddard that there was a need for accurate, reliable information about Pepsi-Cola memorabilia.

With the publication of *Introduction to Pepsi Collecting*, Stoddard realized that he had a full-time job in the promotion of Pepsi collectibles. He quit his job in marketing in 1991, and formed Double Dot Enterprises (Double Dot: a term referring to older Pepsi-Cola trademark logos). His reputation for thorough research, and keen knowledge of antique advertising memorabilia soon led to a consulting agreement with the Pepsi-Cola Company. For the past 15 years, he has traveled throughout the country displaying his collection at Pepsi-Cola sponsored functions. During this time he has written additional books on Pepsi. In 1996, *The Complete Guide To Pepsi-Cola Collectibles* was released, followed by *Pepsi: 100 Years* in 1997, and *Pepsi Now and Then* in 1999. *The Encyclopedia of Pepsi-Cola Collectibles* was published in 2002.

About Pepsi Collecting

Pepsi-Cola memorabilia collectors are among the most dedicated of all collectors. Collecting Pepsi-Cola artifacts is both difficult and challenging. This is due in great part to the turbulent beginning experienced by the Pepsi-Cola Company. Financial difficulties, combined with political and economic conditions, made Pepsi-Cola's first years more about survival than about selling soft drinks. This resulted in limited amounts of Pepsi-Cola advertising materials produced. With two bankruptcies and several moves, much of the material that was produced was either destroyed or lost. This includes most of the records of what was made. Unlike other collectibles, no one can say for certain what Pepsi memorabilia exists. This is truly the most exciting part of being a Pepsi collector. No one knows for certain what's out there. Every time you look for Pepsi stuff, you have a chance of finding something that no collector has ever seen before. The scarcity of Pepsi collectibles results in a higher value of older Pepsi memorabilia.

Within the world of Pepsi collecting, there are many sub-categories. One can specialize in bottles, cans, toys, signs, crowns (bottle caps), or paper. Within these categories, some collectors decide to specialize in a sub-category. For example, a bottle collector may specialize in commemorative bottles. The possibilities are endless of how you can make Pepsi collecting fit your interest.

If you are just getting started, it is important for you to observe some guidelines. Most importantly, you should only buy what you like. Deal only with reputable antique dealers who will guarantee the authenticity of what they are selling in writing. Keep good records of what you buy. In order to ensure that Pepsi collecting will always be fun for you, do not spend more than you can afford.

Meeting other collectors makes the hobby so much more interesting. One of the best ways to do that is through participation in the Pepsi-Cola Collectors Club. This gives you an opportunity to meet other collectors and exchange information.

As a Pepsi collector, you are collecting the artifacts of the Pepsi-Cola Company. In some cases, these artifacts are irreplaceable pieces of Pepsi history, and it is important that you care for them properly. Proper framing of cardboard signs and paper documents will not only aid in preservation, but also add to their beauty. In the long run, taking good care of your Pepsi collection will only add to its value.

One of the most frequently asked questions about Pepsi collecting is "where can I find Pepsi-Cola memorabilia?" The answer is: Everywhere — at yard sales, flea markets, antique stores, and auctions. You can even find Pepsi stuff in your local grocery store. At times, old signs get left in a corner or hidden away — you never know. Ultimately, the best place to enrich your Pepsi collection is Pepsi Fest, an annual event hosted by the Pepsi-Cola Collectors Club.

Condition and Grading

Knowledge about what you are collecting is an important part of the enjoyment of Pepsi collecting. In this, my third book on Pepsi collectibles, the content is expanded to include more information about the original usage and history of Pepsi memorabilia. The field of advertising memorabilia is an exciting one, but can be fraught with pitfalls concerning the price, grading, rarity, and dating of an item. With this book, I hope to help the novice, as well as the experienced collector, in the appraisal and acquisition of Pepsi memorabilia.

In my last Pepsi collecting book, I adopted a rarity scale that has become a standard among Pepsi collectors. To many collectors, the scarcity of an item can be more important than its price. A rare item that is overpriced may be a justifiable purchase. On the other hand, an overpriced, common item could be purchased at another time and perhaps at a better price. The rarity scale ranges from "A" to "E." "A" items are the most common because they were widely produced, generally newer, and inexpensive. "E" items are extremely rare, with only a few known in existence. Most items, you will find, range between the two extremes. This scale should be a factor in what you are willing to pay for a Pepsi-Cola collectible.

In books on collectibles, pricing is always the most controversial aspect. It is necessary that collectors be able to attach a reasonable value to the pieces they own, as well as those they are interested in buying. As with any collectible, it is difficult to do this. Prices rise and fall solely on the basis of supply and demand. I have tried to be as consistent as possible in establishing a hierarchical price structure that values each piece in relation to other pieces of the same age and rarity. Ultimately, the prices in this book should be a guide. Prices change continuously, both rising and falling. The prices given in this book assume that the item is in near mint condition. For any condition less than near mint, the price should be adjusted accordingly.

Grading is an important aspect of pricing. Condition is everything. In valuing advertising collectibles, the visibility of the logo, trademark, etc. is vitally important in establishing price. Buyers should also be aware that missing parts, mechanical dysfunction, and retouching all detract from the value of a piece. Sizes are included to give the reader a perspective of dimension. In most cases, they are rounded to whole numbers for simplicity, and are not meant to be used for purposes of authentication.

Dating Pepsi memorabilia is not an exact science. As much as possible, dates have been derived from Pepsi-Cola corporate documents and paper pieces with original dates. Putting these facts together with what we know about the history of Pepsi advertising (changes in colors, bottle styles, slogans) gives us approximate dates of usage. All dates used in this book are based on first known usage. In other words, an advertising sign may have been produced by Pepsi-Cola for several years, but the dates in this book only reflect when the sign was first issued. In some cases, an individual bottler may have used a trademark or bottle style beyond the period of time authorized by the Pepsi-Cola Company. This is rarely done today, but in the 1930s, 1940s, and 1950s, this was a common practice. The information provided in this book can be useful to accurately date your Pepsi memorabilia.

Appraising advertising memorabilia is often a subjective task, but one that is critical to the informed purchase of a collectible. This book is a guide in making that task easier for Pepsi collectors. To be a successful Pepsi collector, you have to become your own expert.

Reference Guide

Two of the most important factors in determining the value of a Pepsi collectible are condition and rarity. No matter how rare or old something is, if it is faded, cracked, or missing pieces, the value will be negatively affected. Remember, you are buying these items to display. If most of the image is gone, you cannot really enjoy the item. If you come across a very rare piece, you can pay a little more than you thought you would because of its scarcity. Remember, supply and demand is an important part in determining value. The bottom line is that a rare piece in excellent condition will command top dollar.

This cardboard sign, though rare, is in terrible shape, with cracks and missing pieces. You should only buy a piece in this condition if it is inexpensive.

This cardboard sign is rare and in mint condition. Overpaying for a sign like this is very acceptable.

This metal carrier is very common. You should only buy common items in good condition, and pay book value or less. On the scarcity scale, this is an "A" - very common.

Although the condition of this cardboard sign isn't perfect, it is good enough, considering the rarity. On the scarcity scale, this is an E+ - very rare.

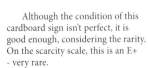

A Brief History Of The Pepsi-Cola Company

Once upon a time, soft drinks were created in the back room of local drug stores. The druggist would try various mixtures of new and exotic ingredients. Most of these new drinks never gained more than local fame, but a few went on to become household names. Pepsi-Cola is one of those drinks that traces its roots back to the corner drugstore. In 1898, Caleb Bradham, of New Bern, North Carolina, invented it.

The Pepsi story is typical of most soft drinks. The local druggist, Bradham, experimenting with different formulas, came up with one that was very popular with the local clientele. The drink was initially nicknamed "Brad's Drink," after the inventor. Soon Bradham believed his creation needed a more marketable name. After all, his drink was developed not only as refreshment, but also as a means to invigorate a tired soul. It is believed that the name Pepsi-Cola is derived from a combination of the words pepsin and cola. Bradham believed that his new drink aided digestion similar to the way the pepsin enzyme does. However, Pepsi never contained pepsin. "Cola" represents the refreshing and invigorating qualities of the drink. By 1900, Pepsi-Cola had become so popular, that Bradham started the Pepsi-Cola Company. At first, the Pepsi-Cola Company simply sold Pepsi-Cola syrup to drug stores in eastern North Carolina.

By 1905, demand for Pepsi-Cola had increased so much that Bradham decided it was time to offer Pepsi-Cola for sale in bottles. To facilitate the sale of Pepsi-Cola in bottles, Bradham issued the first of many franchise agreements. Soon the name of Pepsi-Cola was known throughout the southeastern United States. As 1910 approached, there were nearly 240 Pepsi-Cola bottling franchises. This resulted in the need for the first Pepsi-Cola bottler's convention, which was held in 1910.

One of the reasons for Pepsi-Cola's popularity, besides the good taste, was that it was pure. Unlike many of the other popular drinks of the day, Pepsi did not contain any harmful ingredients. Some of Pepsi's competitors used narcotics and other dangerous substances in their formulas. In 1906, the United States government enacted the Pure Food and Drug Act, which required food and drug companies to remove dangerous ingredients from their products. Pepsi was not required to change their already pure formula. As a result of this act, in 1907, Pepsi began using "pure, food drink" as part of their advertisement.

Bradham was very pleased with this designation, because it was his desire to create a drink that would have no harmful effects. The original Pepsi-Cola formula did not even contain caffeine. Because Pepsi was so healthy for people, it was even advertised as a drink that was safe for children. It was suggested in advertising that Pepsi-Cola would help children grow up healthy.

Sales were now exceeding Bradham's wildest expectations. A new home office was built in 1908. Tens of thousands of dollars were spent promoting Pepsi-Cola. Everything from tip trays to hand fans were given out as advertising premiums to Pepsi-Cola customers. An advertising agency was employed to improve Pepsi advertising. One of their first efforts was to hire famed racecar driver, Barney Oldfield, to endorse Pepsi-Cola.

Success continued for Bradham and Pepsi-Cola between 1910 and 1915. The net income for the Pepsi-Cola Company in 1915 was $31,346. Pepsi-Cola was now being sold in Virginia, North Carolina, South Carolina, Georgia, Florida, Alabama, and Tennessee. At the same time, Bradham was making plans to sell Pepsi-Cola throughout the rest of the United States.

Unfortunately, times were about to get tough for Pepsi-Cola. On June 28th, 1914, Archduke Francis Ferdinand was assassinated in the city of Sarajevo, Bosnia, triggering World War I. Within a few short years, the effects of the war reached New Bern, North Carolina, and Pepsi-Cola. Sugar shortages and price controls decimated the profits of the Pepsi-Cola Company.

Initially, Bradham's biggest problem was finding enough sugar to manufacture Pepsi-Cola syrup. At times, he was forced to use sugar substitutes, which in some cases altered the good taste of Pepsi-Cola. Eventually, this sub-standard Pepsi-Cola would affect the sales substantially. After the conclusion of the war, price controls were lifted, resulting in extremely high sugar prices. The cost of sugar soared from 3 cents per pound, to over 28 cents per pound. With the price of soft drinks well established at 5 cents a bottle or glass, Pepsi had no choice but to absorb the additional cost of sugar. Concerned that the price of sugar would continue to rise, Bradham was forced to purchase a large quantity of sugar at 28 cents per pound. Soon after this purchase, the bottom fell out of the sugar market, with prices tumbling to a pre-war low. This was the final straw that would eventually lead to the bankruptcy of the Pepsi-Cola Company.

Several attempts were made to revive the financially starved Pepsi-Cola Company. One such attempt was made to dissolve the old Pepsi-Cola Company and incorporate a new Pepsi-Cola Company with a new stock offering. This was too little, too late. On May 31, 1923, the Pepsi-Cola Company was certified bankrupt. The assets of the company were eventually sold to the Craven Holding Corporation for $35,000.

Meanwhile, in Richmond, Virginia, the Old Dominion Beverage Company was looking for a replacement for Taka-Kola. The Coca-Cola Company had challenged the Taka-Kola trademark in court. The court ruled in favor of the Coca-Cola Company, forcing the Taka-Kola Company to operate without a cola drink. The owners of the Old Dominion Company met with the Craven Holding Company, and decided that Pepsi-Cola would be a suitable replacement for Taka-Kola. Rather than just sell the Pepsi-Cola formula to Old Dominion, they decided to merge the two companies together to create the Pepsi-Cola Corporation of Richmond, Virginia.

From the beginning, the new Pepsi-Cola Corporation was undercapitalized, causing a succession of financial problems. With these problems came changes within management and investors. By 1928, the Pepsi-Cola Corporation was reorganized into a new company named the National Pepsi-Cola Corporation. The National Pepsi-Cola Corporation tried desperately to regain the former success of Pepsi-Cola. They created new advertising, introduced a new bottle design, and made an all-out effort to recruit new bottlers. Unfortunately, their timing was terrible. On October 29th, 1929, the stock market in the United States crashed. This crash eventually led to the Great Depression, resulting in a serious economic downturn. By May of 1931, Pepsi-Cola was once again bankrupt.

In New York, Charles Guth, president of Loft Candy, was in a bitter dispute with Coca-Cola over the wholesale price of Coca-Cola syrup. Loft operated over 130 soda fountains in the greater New York area. Guth believed that with that kind of volume, Loft deserved better pricing. Coca-Cola believed that Guth had no choice but to buy their syrup, and refused to offer any discount. Guth, unaccustomed to being told no, decided to replace Coca-Cola at his soda fountains. Word reached Guth that the trademark and formula for Pepsi-Cola was being sold in a bankruptcy sale. He decided that Pepsi-Cola would make the perfect soft drink for Loft soda fountains. In 1931, Guth purchased the trademark and formula for the sum of $9,600, thus making Loft the new parent company of Pepsi-Cola.

After refinement of the Pepsi-Cola formula at the Loft laboratories, Pepsi-Cola was ready for distribution to the soda fountains. Despite advertising and a competitive price, New York was not ready for this drink from North Carolina. After several years of struggling, there was no significant increase in sales of Pepsi-Cola at the Loft Drug stores. After several attempts to increase sales, Guth decided to sell Pepsi-Cola in a fancy 12-ounce bottle for ten cents. Pepsi's prospects went from bad to worse. With their backs to the wall, it was time for a daring move. The price of Pepsi-Cola was reduced from 10 cents a bottle to 5 cents for a 12-ounce bottle. With most of the competition selling a 6-ounce bottle for a nickel, this was a bargain that New Yorkers could not pass up. Overnight, Pepsi-Cola became an instant success.

Guth realized he had a winner and moved quickly to set up bottling operations across America. With just a handful of bottlers in 1934, the number grew to 315 Pepsi-Cola bottlers in 1939. Once again, Pepsi-Cola was on the rise, surpassing all previous successes. Unfortunately, as Pepsi-Cola's prospects increased, Loft Candy fortunes took a severe downturn. Believing that Pepsi-Cola had more potential than Loft, Guth left the candy company, taking Pepsi-Cola with him. This began a multi-year court battle between Loft and Guth over the legal rights to Pepsi-Cola. In 1939, Loft prevailed. Pepsi-Cola was once again part of Loft. Shortly thereafter, Loft changed its name to Pepsi-Cola, and liquidated all of the assets of the candy business. This created the new Pepsi-Cola Company.

During the court battles with Guth, Loft had run out of money. In desperate need of cash, they turned to Phoenix securities, a firm that specialized in helping companies on the verge of going out of business. In exchange for much needed cash, Phoenix received a percentage of the Loft Company, and a seat on the board of directors. Phoenix selected Walter Mack to become part of the Loft board. In 1939, Walter Mack was made the president of the Pepsi-Cola Company. Mack soon took total control of Pepsi-Cola—everything from production to advertising. Aware of the importance of advertising in the soft drink business, Mack made an all-out effort to improve Pepsi-Cola advertising. The three most important promotions at this time were the adoption of the Pepsi-Cola jingle to be used in all Pepsi advertising, the creation of Pepsi and Pete, the Pepsi-Cola Cops, and skywriting. Pepsi-Cola was the first to use skywriting as an advertising medium. This new advertising campaign helped to increase Pepsi sales and make consumers more aware of the big nickel drink. The future could not have looked better for Pepsi-Cola. Sadly, a new problem was on the horizon—World War II.

World War II brought new challenges for Pepsi-Cola. Sugar, a key ingredient in Pepsi-Cola, was now being rationed. The rationing rules favored companies that had been in business for a long time. Most Pepsi bottlers were just getting started. Added to this problem were gasoline rationing, material shortages, and manpower shortages. Many Pepsi bottlers left their businesses to enlist in the military. Mack was not the type of person that easily gave up. He went about trying to find ways to solve each of these problems. One of his most interesting solutions was "El Masco," sugar syrup designed to circumvent the sugar importation rules of World War II. This, along with many other ingenious solutions to problems kept the bottlers in operation. With hard work and luck, Pepsi survived World War II.

Pepsi-Cola management believed that the end of the war cleared the way for Pepsi to once again begin its quest to becoming the number one cola drink. Post-war inflation, however, had a devastating effect on this goal. Too many dollars and too few products caused escalating prices. Unfortunately, Pepsi-Cola had advertised their nickel drink so much, that they were forced to try to hold the price at 5 cents. With their competitor selling a 6-ounce bottle for 5 cents, Pepsi's profit margin had always been thin. Now that margin was gone. In order to survive, something had to be done. Some bottlers raised their price from 5 cents to 6 cents. Other bottlers switched to a 10-ounce bottle for 5 cents. All efforts to regain Pepsi's previous success were unfruitful. By 1950, Pepsi-Cola was once again on the brink of bankruptcy.

Mack had fought hard to maintain the 5-cent price of Pepsi. Many bottlers resented this, because the bargain price came at the cost of their profits. The conflict between Mack and the bottlers led to the board of directors deciding to make a change in the leadership. In 1951, Mack was elevated to chairman of the board, and Alfred Steele became the new president of the Pepsi-Cola Company. Steele had been a vice-president with the Coca-Cola Company. Known for his leadership and showmanship qualities, Steele's mission was to resurrect Pepsi once again.

Steele's first goal was to make Pepsi-Cola a professional company. He felt that Pepsi lacked a consistent image nationwide. In many cases, the taste changed from region to region. He was determined to have all the bottlers use the same advertising, get the drivers to wear the same uniform, and most importantly, get the same Pepsi taste from one city to the next.

His biggest challenge was the image of Pepsi-Cola. The resurgence of Pepsi began during the Great Depression. The 12-ounce bottle for 5 cents became known as the bargain drink. In the postwar prosperity of America, a bargain drink was not as desirable as it had been during less prosperous times.

Additionally, American taste had changed. Excessively sweet drinks became less popular. To meet these challenges, Steele had Pepsi-Cola reformulated to contain less sugar. The advertising campaign that accompanied this new formula was "Pepsi-Cola, The Light Refreshment." The ad campaign was complete with magazine and billboard ads featuring young, attractive men and women enjoying Pepsi-Cola.

The changes instituted by Steele paid off immediately. By 1955, sales had more than doubled. Once again, Pepsi was back on track. Steele's leadership continued to guide Pepsi-Cola's growth throughout the 1950s. By 1959, sales hit an all time record of 13 million; ten times what it was in 1950. To further improve Pepsi's public image, a new bottle was introduced in 1958. The new "swirl" bottle replaced the bottle Pepsi had used since 1940. Along with the bottle, came a new advertising campaign—"Be Sociable, Have a Pepsi."

In 1959, Steele embarked on a tour to promote Pepsi's new advertising to the bottlers. The stress and exhaustion of this high-powered tour resulted in Steele suffering a fatal heart attack. The man that was responsible for modernizing Pepsi-Cola was suddenly gone, leaving a leadership void that would be difficult to fill. Even today, many of the bottlers still credit Al Steele with turning Pepsi-Cola around and making it a modern soft drink company.

One of Steele's most important accomplishments was to change the focus of Pepsi advertising from the product to image; in other words, he advocated selling the "sizzle," not the steak. During the 1960s, advertising was designed to enhance the image of Pepsi, including the highly successful "Pepsi Generation" campaign. Finally, the image of Pepsi as the bargain drink was eradicated once and for all.

The 1960s saw a major change in the way all companies, including Pepsi, advertised. The growing popularity of television gave advertisers an abundant audience to hear about their products. As the popularity of television increased, so did the advertising rates. Eventually, television spots received the largest share of the Pepsi-Cola advertising budget. This resulted in less money being spent on advertising signage. The golden age of Pepsi point-of-purchase advertising was over.

In 1963, Donald Kendall became president of the Pepsi-Cola Company. Kendall first received prominence within the Pepsi organization in 1959. At that time, he was president of Pepsi International. At a trade expo in Moscow, Kendall had convinced then vice-president Richard Nixon to get the former USSR premiere, Nikita Khrushchev, to visit the Pepsi exhibit at the expo. When Khrushchev stopped to sample Pepsi, all the press photographers snapped pictures. The next day, the headlines around the world read "Khrushchev Gets Sociable." The headline referred to the advertising slogan "Be Sociable, Have a Pepsi."

While president of the Pepsi-Cola Company, Kendall spearheaded the effort to create Diet Pepsi, and negotiate the purchase of Mountain Dew from Tip Corporation. Despite this, most considered his biggest accomplishment was his successful merger between Frito-Lay and Pepsi-Cola to form PepsiCo in 1965. Finally, Pepsi was established as one of the great American consumer product companies.

Now able to compete on equal footing with the Coca-Cola Company, Pepsi-Cola has earned its way as a legitimate soft drink company. With promotions such as the Pepsi Challenge, Pepsi has, at times, been able to outsell their long-time nemesis. In 1985, Coca-Cola changed their original formula to become more like Pepsi, resulting in Pepsi's declaration that they had won the cola war.

Today, Pepsi-Cola is considered to be a total beverage company, selling everything from Pepsi-Cola to iced tea. The dream of Caleb Bradham, to sell the public a refreshing drink, continues. Pepsi-Cola products are now available in over 186 countries around the world.

Trademarks

Throughout the history of the Pepsi-Cola Company, a number of trademarks were used to represent the cola company. Knowing when each trademark was used is key to identifying the age of Pepsi-Cola memorabilia. Most of the time, this information will help you correctly date your Pepsi-Cola memorabilia. However, there are occasions when this may not be the most accurate way to date your Pepsi items, as trademarks were used at times beyond the date the company started using a new version.

Identified in this section are the major trademark changes. There are numerous minor variations to many Pepsi-Cola trademarks that are not shown here. Overall, this should be an aid in identifying Pepsi memorabilia. There is no way to be 100 percent accurate, but with the use of this chart and the dates slogans were used, you should be very close most of the time.

1898 - This is considered by most to be the first Pepsi-Cola trademark. Unfortunately, there is no evidence that this trademark was ever used by Caleb Bradham. It is alleged that this logo was designed by a local artist. My guess is that this design was the model for the Pepsi trademark that was eventually used.

1903 - Similar to the first logo, this trademark was actually used in a newspaper advertisement in 1903. This logo was the first to incorporate advertising information into the design. Some characteristics were adopted from the 1898 logo, but overall this was a new design.

1906 - This trademark was registered with the United States Patent Office on August 7, 1906. This logo appears to be the 1903 logo, but more streamlined and modernized. We now see a logo that is similar to the double dot script used for most of Pepsi-Cola's first fifty years.

1909 -By this time, the trademark had evolved into a logo that symbolized a modern, professional company. This logo, with minor variations, was used by Pepsi-Cola from 1909 through 1950.

1939 -This is a refinement of the 1909 trademark, with a significant new characteristic. The trademark now features a thick blue line
around the Pepsi-Cola letters. This line was primarily used in 1939.
However, you can find it on some memorabilia in later years.

1940 - This trademark, introduced in 1940, was nicknamed the
flag logo for obvious reasons. Essentially, it incorporated the standard
script logo into a flag background. It is important to notice that the
script logo is balanced by the wave design in the flag. This was the
beginning of making the trademark more than just the script logo.

1943 - The flag logo evolved into an oval logo, giving the white
wave background a more dynamic look. This is an important transi-
tion, because this design would become the genesis of the crown logo.

1945 - The crown logo, taken from the Pepsi-Cola bottle cap, replaced the oval as Pepsi's primary icon. Looking at the center of the bottle cap, you can see remnants of the flag as well as the oval logo. Also, at this time, red, white and blue became the corporate colors of the Pepsi-Cola Company.

1951 - In the 1950s, Pepsi decided to modernize their image. One step in doing this was to give the trademark a face-lift. Therefore, in 1951, Pepsi made one of the biggest changes in their logo since the days of Caleb Bradham. The double dot script was replaced by a sleek, more modern-looking single dot script.

1951 -At the same time, the crown logo was redesigned to incorporate the new single dot script. The new crown trademark tilted slightly to the right, but was definitely the descendant of the 1945 crown. The single dot crown logo became the predominant Pepsi symbol in the 1950s.

1963 - A new decade began with many changes going on in our society. To reflect this new era, the Pepsi logo was once again updated. The image of the crown was less defined, and the familiar Pepsi-Cola script was replaced with block letters.

1965 - The 1963 logo update turned out to be short-lived. By 1965, the trademark was once again changed. The crown part of the logo completely disappeared. Only the wave, first developed in 1943, remained. The emphasis on Pepsi-Cola's name had changed to just "Pepsi."

1971 - In time for Pepsi's 75th anniversary, a new trademark was introduced. The logo featured Pepsi framed by the wave on the top and bottom, with what appears to be bookends on each side. This logo became known as the "bookend" logo. The logo consisted of the red, white, and blue look that Pepsi had first adopted in 1945. Additionally, a lighter shade of blue was included.

1987 - A variation of the bookend logo with new block print. The block print used since 1963 was replaced by a new style- most notably the rounded "E."

1991 - The modified crown logo becomes secondary in the trademark to the block print. The name Pepsi is the featured part of this '90s logo.

1996 - The circle is complete. The crown logo is once again the predominant Pepsi trademark, modernized and named the "globe," but still bearing the essential characteristics that were first created in 1940. If you go back and look at the 1940 flag logo, you can see the roots of the globe logo.

1998 - The globe and the Pepsi-Cola letters are married together, forming a more traditional-looking trademark. The important feature of this trademark is the blue background, which, during the 1990s, became the corporate color of Pepsi-Cola.

Pepsi-Cola Advertising Slogans

1903: Exhilarating, Invigorating, Aids Digestion

1907: Original Pure Food Drink

1908: Delicious and Healthful

1915: For All Thirsts - Pepsi-Cola

1919: Pepsi-Cola - It Makes You Scintillate

1920: Drink Pepsi-Cola - It Will Satisfy You

1928: Peps You Up!

1929: Here's Health!

1932: Sparkling, Delicious

1933: It's the Best Cola Drink

1934: Double Size

1934: Refreshing and Healthful

1938: Join the Swing to Pepsi-Cola

1939 Twice as Much for a Nickel

1943: Bigger Drink, Better Taste

1947: It's a Great American Custom

1949: Why Take Less When Pepsi's Best

1950: More Bounce to the Ounce

1954: The Light Refreshment

1958: Be Sociable, Have a Pepsi

1961: Now It's Pepsi for Those Who Think Young

1963: Come Alive! You're in the Pepsi Generation

1967: Taste that Beats the Others Cold. Pepsi Pours It On

1969: You've Got a Lot to Live. Pepsi's Got a Lot to Give

1973: Join the Pepsi People Feelin' Free

1976: Have a Pepsi Day

1979: Catch that Pepsi Spirit

1981: Pepsi's Got Your Taste for Life

1983: Pepsi Now!

1984: The Choice of a New Generation

1992: Gotta Have It

1993: Be Young, Have Fun, Drink Pepsi

1995: Nothing Else is a Pepsi

1997: Generation Next

1999: The Joy of Cola

2001: The Joy of Pepsi

SIGNS

During the first half of the twentieth century, signage was an important part of Pepsi-Cola's advertising program. Before television, advertising signs were key to remind customers to drink Pepsi-Cola. There was a battle to get signs in the most visible locations in every mom and pop grocery store across America. For this reason, a number of different shapes and styles of signs were created, including signs that were to be used exclusively indoors, and others that were to be used outside. Some of these signs were made to fit under windows, and others on screen doors. The main objective was to place signs in strategic locations, where consumers would be sure to notice them. With the advances in technology, and increased competition, signs became more sophisticated. This resulted in everything from neon signs to multicolored, three-dimensional cardboard signs.

To help make cardboard signs more attractive, Pepsi employed some of the best artists available, including Rolf Armstrong, George Petty, and Zoe Mozert. If you own a Pepsi-Cola memorabilia done by any of these artists, you own a piece of art.

For the Pepsi-Cola Company, the years between 1930 and 1960 were the golden years of advertising signage. During this time, Pepsi produced some of their best, and no doubt most collectible advertising signs. This period represents the bulk of Pepsi-Cola advertising signage. If you collect Pepsi-Cola memorabilia, it is more than likely that your collection will include a significant number of items from this era.

The signs in this section have been arbitrarily designated into categories. These designations are done for convenience, and have no official standing. Many of these signs could easily fit into two or three different categories. The nomenclature used to identify different styles and types of signs is based on soft drink industry standards.

DIE-CUT CARDBOARD

1905   E+ $2,500
6" x 24"

1905 $2,000
Double Sided 9" Tall

DIE-CUT

Die-cut refers to using a die during the printing process to cut a sign to a specific shape. Most die-cut cardboard signs have easels attached to the back so they may sit on a counter or be displayed on a wall. These signs are some of the most outstanding point-of-purchase material produced by the Pepsi-Cola Company. Because of their beauty, die-cut Pepsi signs are in high demand, and command premium value.

DIE-CUT CARDBOARD

1936   D+ $750
Easel Back   5" x 16"

1936   D+ $1,000
Easel Back   10" x 16"

DIE-CUT CARDBOARD

◄

1936   D+ $1,500
23" x 26"

1936   D $1,000
Easel Back 19" x 15"

◄

DIE-CUT CARDBOARD

◄

1936   E $800
8" x 19"

►

1943   E $300
Display 11" x 17"

DIE-CUT CARDBOARD

1940   E $1,000
10" x 13"

DIE-CUT CARDBOARD

1943   D+ $250
   5" x 8"

1945   E $900
   12" x 18"

DIE-CUT CARDBOARD

1943   E $300
Double-Sided
11" x 12"

◄   1947   E $800
8" x 18"

DIE-CUT CARDBOARD

1951   D+ $150
11" x 14"

1950   D+ $350
14" x 21"

DIE-CUT CARDBOARD

1954   C+ $65
13" x 19"

DIE-CUT CARDBOARD

1954   C+ $65

18" x 20"

DIE-CUT CARDBOARD

◄

1954   C+ $65

12" x 20"

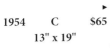

►

1954   C $65

13" x 19"

DIE-CUT CARDBOARD

1954   C+ $65
18" x 20"

DIE-CUT CARDBOARD

1954   C+ $75
18" x 20"

1949   E $800
Easel Back 14" x 26"

DIE-CUT CARDBOARD

1954   C+ $85
18" x 20"

1949   E $800
Easel Back 14" x 26"

DIE-CUT CARDBOARD

1951   D $400 ▲
19" x 21"

▶

1959   C+ $150
Easel Back 74" Tall

FIVE GORGEOUS GIRLS

"Five Gorgeous Girls" was the name that was used to identify these five cardboard images. They were introduced in 1949. At that time, the Pepsi bottler paid $2.00 per set for these beautiful cardboard signs. Because of their beauty and rarity, they have become very popular among collectors of antique advertising. It is difficult to find the whole set together, but that is the fun of collecting!

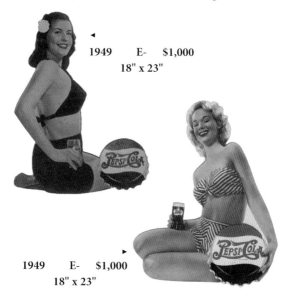

◄   1949   E- $1,000
18" x 23"

1949   E- $1,000   ►
18" x 23"

FIVE GORGEOUS GIRLS

◄ 1949   E- $1,000
        18" x 23"

▲ 1949   E- $1,000
        17" x 38"

▲ 1949   E- $1,000
        14" x 38"

DIE-CUT CARDBOARD

1940   D+ $1,600
    29" x 40"

1936   D+ $800
    10" x 32"

DIE-CUT CARDBOARD

◄

1951　　C+　　$350
Easel Back 24" x 25"

►

1943　　D+　　$650
Easel Back 28" x 33"

DIE-CUT CARDBOARD

1948   D+ $400 ▲
3-D 28" x 26"

◄

1943   D $450
21" Dia.

DIE-CUT CARDBOARD

▲ 1943   D+ $500
   Easel Back 30" x 21

1943   D $350
   21" x 24"

DIE-CUT CARDBOARD

1947   E+ $2,500
Easel Back 30" x 68"

1987   B- $25
Easel Back 72" Tall

DIE-CUT CARDBOARD

1905   E+ $9,000
20" x 34"

CARDBOARD

1905   E+ $1,500
Paper 11" x 17"

RARE LITHOGRAPHS

Represented on these pages are some of the rarest and most sought after Pepsi-Cola collectibles. Created by some of the best illustrators of the time, these signs are classics. Sadly, lithographed cardboard signs, if not kept in optimum conditions, will deteriorate over time. For this reason, only a limited number of these signs survived. If you have have an opportunity to buy one of these signs and can afford it, don't hesitate about the investment.

CARDBOARD

◄ 1907   E+ $12,000
       10" x 12.5"

► 1907   E+ $10,000
       10" x 12.5"

CARDBOARD

◄

1909　　E+　$5,500
　　20" x 25"

1909　D+　$3,500
　　25" x 31"

►

CARDBOARD

1909   E+ $6,000
18" x 24"

THREE-DIMENSIONAL SELF-FRAMED

These signs represent some of Pepsi-Cola's finest point of purchase advertising from the 1940s. These beautiful Pepsi girls are surrounded by a three-dimensional cardboard frame that is part of the sign. Because of the fragile construction of these signs, it is rare to find them in good condition. For this reason, it is recommended that if you find any of these signs in good shape, purchase it.

◄

1940   D+ $1,600
Cardboard 24" x 34"

►

1943   D+ $1,600
Cardboard 24" x 34"

THREE-DIMENSIONAL SELF-FRAMED

◄

1943   D+ $1,600
Cardboard 24" x 31"

►

1943   D+ $1,600
Cardboard 25" x 35"

CARDBOARD

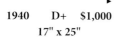

◄

1943   D $600
      28" x 35"

►

1940   D+ $1,000
      17" x 25"

CARDBOARD

▲ 1950   D $600
Self-Framed 27" x 21"

▲ 1950   D $600
Self-Framed 27" x 21"

CARDBOARD

◄

1941   D $600
Easel Back 18" x 26"

►

1940   C+ $350
18" x 27"

CARDBOARD

▲ 1940   C+ $400
George Petty 21" x 11"

▲ 1940   C+ $400
21" x 11"

CARDBOARD

▲ 1940　　C-　　$450
30" x 13"

▲ 1940　　C+　　$350
12" x 6"

CARDBOARD

◄ 1943   D $75
    11" x 14"

    1945   D $100   ►
      11" x 14"

CARDBOARD

◄ 1951   C+ $75
      11" x 14"

1951   C+ $85 ▶
    19" x 21"

CARDBOARD

◄
1945   D $125
  11" x 14"

1951   C- $35
    11" x 14"   ►

CARDBOARD

1951   C $85
      19" x 21"

1956   C $50
      11" x 14"

CARDBOARD

◄

1951　　C　　$85
　　19" x 21"

►

1951　　C+　　$85
　　19" x 21"

CARDBOARD INSERTS

Inserts are cardboard signs that were produced to fit into frames. At first, wood frames were used, followed by metal frames. Previous to this, these types of signs were called tackers, because they were actually tacked to the walls. It was believed that the signs placed in frames would receive better recognition. The frames also helped preserve and protect the cardboard. These inserts were produced in two sizes. The large inserts were 37" x 25". The small inserts were 28" x 11". Any sign with different measurements was most likely designed as a tacker, car, bus, or trolley sign, rather than an insert sign.

1945   D+ $900
Easel Back 37" x 25"

CARDBOARD INSERTS

▲ 1949   D $850
37" x 25" Metal Frame

▲ 1949   D $850
37" x 25" Wood Frame

CARDBOARD INSERTS

▲ 1950   C+ $500
37" x 25"

▲ 1951   C+ $300
37" x 25"

CARDBOARD INSERTS

▲ 1945   D+ $900
37" x 25"

▲ 1950   C+ $500
37" x 25" Metal Frame

CARDBOARD INSERTS

▲ 1951   D- $500
37" x 25"

▲ 1954   C $175
Double-Sided 37" x 25"

CARDBOARD INSERTS

▲ 1954   C $125
37" x 25"

▲ 1954   C $175
Double-Sided
37" x 25"

CARDBOARD INSERTS

▲ 1954   C $175
Double-Sided 37" x 25"

▲ 1954   C $175
Double-Sided 37" x 25"

CARDBOARD INSERTS

◄

1970   C+ $100
      22" x 28"

►

1958   C $125
      37" x 25"

CARDBOARD INSERTS

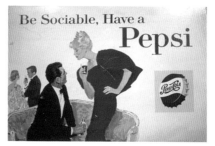

▲ 1958   C $125

37" x 25"

▲ 1954   C $175

Double-Sided 37" x 25"

CARDBOARD INSERTS

◄ 1963   B $45
  25" x 37"

► 1964   B $45
  25" x 37"

CARDBOARD INSERTS

▲ 1940   D $500
28" x 11"

▲ 1943   D- $450
28" x 11"

CARDBOARD INSERTS

▲ 1943   D $500
28" x 11"

▲ 1943   D $500
28" x 11"

CARDBOARD INSERTS

▲ 1943   D $500
28" x 11"

▲ 1945   D $500
28" x 11"

CARDBOARD INSERTS

▲ 1945   D- $450
28" x 11"

▲ 1945   D $500
28" x 11"

CARDBOARD INSERTS

▲ 1947　　D　　$500
28" x 11" Wood Frame

▲ 1949　　D　　$500
28" x 11"

CARDBOARD INSERTS

▲ 1954   B $75
28" x 11"

▲ 1954   B $75
28" x 11"

CARDBOARD INSERTS

▲ 1954   B $75
28" x 11"

▲ 1958   B $75
28" x 11" Metal Frame

CARDBOARD INSERTS

▲ 1960   C $75
28" x 11"

▲ 1964   B $30
28" x 11"

CARDBOARD INSERTS

▲ 1961   B $20
28" x 11"

▲ 1964   B $30
28" x 11"

CARDBOARD INSERTS

▲ 1967   B $30
28" x 11"

▲ 1971   B $30
28" x 11"

CARDBOARD INSERTS

▲ 1971   B $30
28" x 11"

▲ 1976   B $20
28" x 11"

NEON CLOCKS

Clocks are among the oldest and most popular of advertising signage. Most retail stores were eager to hang a clock in their establishment. Clocks have been used as a way to advertise consumer products for decades, and the reason is obvious: Every time you look up to see the time, you see the advertisement. There is no accurate record of when Pepsi-Cola began advertising on clocks. It wasn't until 1940 that this form of advertising became a regular practice for the Pepsi-Cola Company. Within the clock category, there are two that have become very popular among collectors of advertising—neon and double glass clocks.

1939   E $4,200

NEON CLOCKS

1939　　E　　$4,000

1939　　D　　$3,800
Neon 18" x 18"

NEON CLOCK

◄

1945   D $1,800
Neon 18" x 18"

►

1940   E $500
Wood Frame 15" x 15"

CLOCKS

1940   C $250
   15" x 15"

1947   C+ $300
   14" x 14"

CLOCKS

1960   C+ $1,000
Neon 35" Dia.

1951   D $450
17" Dia.

CLOCKS

1951   C+ $1,000
Neon 35" Dia.

1951   E $750
Light-Up 25" x 17"

CLOCKS

◄

1960   D- $1,000
Double Glass 19" Dia.

1954   D+ $500
Plastic 15" Dia.

CLOCKS

1960   C+ $85
  Light-Up 16" x 12"

1964   B+ $75
  16" x 16"

CLOCKS

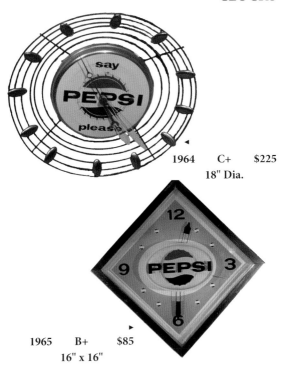

1964   C+ $225
18" Dia.

1965   B+ $85
16" x 16"

CORBUF

1951   D- $75
30" x 60"

CORBUF

Corbuf is single-face, corrugated cardboard. It is used at special events and to decorate displays. It is produced in 250' long rolls with varying heights. Each design is repeated every so many feet. To have a complete corrugated sign, you would need to have the entire design on one sheet.

CORBUF

▲ 1954　　C+　　$25
30" x 48"

▲ 1965　　C　　$20
24" x 36"

DECALS

1936   D $350

7" x 4"

DECALS

Decals are among the most colorful of Pepsi signs. You will find decals in two forms—used and unused. The used are generally placed on glass to enable good viewing. This does not detract from the value. The unused will still be attached to the original backing. Occasionally, the image is face down on the backing material, making viewing impossible until the decal is transferred onto glass. Be careful with the water-transfer decals that are unused. Removing them from the backing is sometimes difficult and they can be damaged. You need to consider this when you are trying to determine how much to pay for an untransferred decal.

DECALS

1937   D+ $500
Double-Sided 10"

1948   D $600
19" x 15"

DECALS

▲ 1945   D $500
9" x 8"

◄

1943   D+ $400
10" Dia.

DECALS

1951   D $75
12" Dia.

1950   D+ $300
10" x 12"

DECALS

1950 E $225
15" Tall

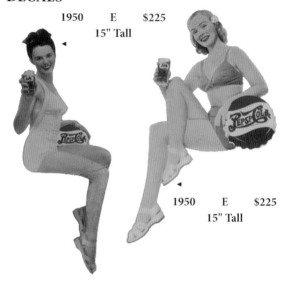

1950 E $225
15" Tall

The five gorgeous girls were issued as decals and as cardboard signs. Either way, they are extremely hard to find. The decals were on one sheet, perforated for easy removal. These are found as single decals, or more rarely as a complete set.

DECALS

1950　　E　　$225
5" Tall

1950　　E　　$225
5" Tall

1950　　E　　$225
5" Tall

DECALS

1951   D $50
10 " x 12"

▲ 1954   C+ $150
16" x 9"

DECALS

▲ 1960   C+ $50
9" x 7"

1965   C+ $35
8" x 5"

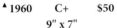

DECALS

1967   C $65
12" x 11"

▲1954   C+ $65
9" x 7"

DISPLAYS

This set of cardboard signs is known as a "festoon" (a decorative chain or strip hanging between two points). This is one of the rarest Pepsi signs known to exist. The sign consists of five, three-dimensional cardboard pieces linked together by a red and white cord. It is most likely that you will find individual pieces of the festoon, rather than the complete festoon. If you do, it is recommended that you buy the pieces, because even the individual pieces are rare.

▲ 1943   E+ $3,800
96" x 48"

DISPLAYS

▲ 1954   D- $225
Corrugated 96" x 32"

▲ 1954   C+ $50
5 Pieces Linked by Wire

DISPLAYS

1983   B+ $75

54" Tall

This is a battery-operated, rotating display.

BOTTLE DISPLAYS

1939   D $350
Foil Coated 14" Tall

BOTTLE DISPLAYS

Bottle displays were used in what was called the cold bottle market. Normally, these were mom and pop stores, where people stopped in to get a cold drink. There are primarily two styles of bottle displays. One is where the bottle slips into the display, the other is where the display slides onto the neck of the bottle. Both styles are equally popular among collectors, which is reflected in their value. These signs are a great way to display old Pepsi bottles.

BOTTLE DISPLAYS

◄

1936   E $550
    13" Tall

1928   E $950
    13" Tall

►

BOTTLE DISPLAYS

1940   D- $750
12" x 14"

1939   D- $350
Foil Coated 14" Tall

BOTTLE DISPLAYS

◄

1940　　D-　　$275
6" Tall

►

1940　　D　　$125
6" x 8"

BOTTLE DISPLAYS

▲ 1957   D $450
16" x 20"

◄
1957   D+ $500
16" x 68"

BOTTLE DISPLAYS

◄

1954   D+ $200
Light-Up 18" Tall

1983   C+ $50
14" Tall

►

RACKS AND RACK SIGNS

Metal racks were given to dealers as a way to increase orders and to get more display space. The popularity of these type of racks disappeared with the returnable bottles. It is very common to find rack signs only. Very often, the sign was removed from the rack and the rack was discarded. These display racks are very popular with collectors for displaying Pepsi collections.

1940   D $400
36" x 35"

RACKS AND RACK SIGNS

◄ 1934   C+ $125
Double-Sided 8" x 8"

▲ 1940   C $200
Double-Sided 16" x 6"

RACKS AND RACK SIGNS

◄ 1940   D+ $300
Door Push 3" x 10"

1940   D $300 ►
Door Push 3" x 10"

▲ 1940   E- $350
Porcelain 35"

FOIL-COATED CARDBOARD

▲ 1954   D $65
Flower Display 10" x 8"

▲ 1965   C $25
14" x 6"

FOIL-COATED CARDBOARD

1967   C $75
13" x 12"

1965   C $45
15" x 13"

FOIL-COATED CARDBOARD

▲ 1960   A $15
12" x 5"

▲ 1960   C $35
11" x 5"

FLANGE SIGNS

Flange signs are normally double-sided. They were used in key locations, where they could be viewed from both sides. Flange signs were used indoors and outdoors. For most collectors, flange signs are highly desirable, and demand premium prices.

1940   D+ $900
Metal 17" x 16"

FLANGE SIGNS

1940   C+ $550
  Metal 15" x 10"

1945   C+ $450
  Masonite 13" x 12"

FLANGE SIGNS

▲ 1951   D- $450
Masonite 44" x 16"

◄

1945   D- $750
17" x15"

FLANGE SIGNS

1951   C+ $450
Metal 15" x 14"

◄

◄

1963   C+ $350
Metal 18" x 15"

GLASS SIGNS

1943   D $400
Printed Reverse 10" x 5"

GLASS SIGNS

Glass signs are made by reverse printing on glass. This process creates a beautiful and attractive product. This is especially true when the printing is backed with the silver that produces mirrors. Due to the fragile nature of glass signs, these are the rarest and most difficult of Pepsi signs to find. Most often these were used at fountain locations or back bar displays.

GLASS SIGNS

◄
1937　　E　　$4,000
Reverse Foil 12" x 10"

▲ 1943　　D　　$300
Printed Reverse 19" x 9"

ADVERTISING MIRRORS

The key to a good advertising sign is to attract the attention of potential customers. Over the years, mirrors have done this as well as any other form of indoor signage. Pepsi advertising mirrors have become some of the most attractive signage offered by the company, thus, a popular choice for advertising at point of sale locations.

Mirrors are very popular to the collector because of their beauty and rarity. The rarity of Pepsi mirrors exists primarily for two reasons. The primary reason is the fragile nature of the glass. Secondly, the silver used to make mirrors tends to deteriorate over time, rendering the mirrors useless.

For all these reasons, Pepsi advertising mirrors make great collectibles.

▲ 1940   E $1,200
14" x 10"

ADVERTISING MIRRORS

▲ 1940   E $650
10" x 20"

▲ 1945   D $250
4" x 12"

ILLUMINATED SIGNS

Illuminated signs, also known as light-up signs, are among the most expensive of Pepsi-Cola collectibles. This is due, in part, to the popularity of light-up signs among collectors. In this category, there is a myriad of different types. There are neon, rotating, glass, plastic, and double-sided signs. They all serve different purposes. Among these types, neon and rotating signs are the most sought-after.

1940   E $1,500
Revolving Light 16" x 10"

ILLUMINATED SIGNS

▲ 1940   D+ $700
13" x 9"

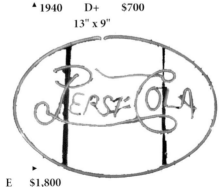

▶
1941   E $1,800
Neon

ILLUMINATED SIGNS

1951   D $350
   Plastic 8" x 8"

1940   E $3,000
   Glass 14" x 7"

ILLUMINATED SIGNS

▲ 1951   E- $2,500
21" x 10"

◄ 1956   C $100
18" x 14"

ILLUMINATED SIGNS

▲ 1954   C+ $250
Plastic 60" x 12"

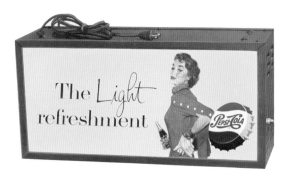

▲ 1954   C+ $275
Plastic 19" x 9"

ILLUMINATED SIGNS

▲ 1954   C+ $450
21" x 7"

▲ 1954   D $1,500
Double-Sided 24" x 18"

ILLUMINATED SIGNS

1954   D $350
      10" x 13" Rotates

1954   D $350
      10" x 13" Rotates

ILLUMINATED SIGNS

1964   C+ $475
Light/Clock 26" x 26"

1963   D+ $800
Rotating 16" Tall

MENU BOARDS

Menu boards are among the few advertising signs that actually serve a function. They were placed in restaurants, grocery stores, and gas stations, where besides advertising Pepsi-Cola, they could list prices or specials. Because of this, they were very popular among Pepsi vendors. To meet this demand, Pepsi produced various styles. Some are strictly menu boards, while others are slate boards that can be used to write on. Menu boards are available in wood, metal, and glass. They range in price from inexpensive to very expensive.

1940   D+ $450 ▲
20" x 30"

▲ 1945   C+ $250
15" x 23"

MENU BOARDS

◄
1951   C $175
20" x 30"

►
1965   B+ $50
20" x 30"

MENU BOARDS

▲ 1954   C+ $350

Glass 36" x 20"

▲ 1954   C+ $175

Light-Up 30" x 24"

METAL

▲ 1940   C+ $350
14" x 5"

▲ 1936   D $400
17" x 6"

METAL

1951   C+ $175
12" x 15"

1950   D+ $425
Kick Plate 11" Tall

METAL

▲ 1909   D+ $600
16" x 8"

▲ 1939   D $350
23" x 12"

METAL

▲ 1939   D- $550
28" x 20"

1945   C+ $250
28" x 20"

METAL

1945   D+ $900
Die-Cut 29" Tall

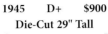

1936   D+ $750
16" x 49"

METAL

1940   D $800
96" x 48"

METAL

▲ 1951   C $250
50" x 36"

▲ 1954   C+ $200
72" x 36"

METAL

▲ 1965   C+ $225
40" x 36"

▲ 1969   B $75
38" x 60"

METAL

▲ 1910   E $7,000
39" x 14"

▲ 1936   D+ $1,800
36" x 24"

METAL

1950   D- $300
27" x 27"

1960   C+ $200
27" x 30"

METAL

◄ 1958   D $800
12 Feet Tall

► 1954   D+ $2,000
30" x 64"

CURB STAND SIGNS

1940   D $500
Display/Frame 20" x 28"

CURB STAND SIGNS

Curb stand signs were designed to fit in a frame that was set out on a sidewalk. Each frame normally held two signs back to back. This enabled a passerby to see the Pepsi sign from both directions. Additionally, curb stand signs were made bearing different phrases. Over the years, most of these frames were discarded, while many of the signs survived. To find these signs in a frame is very rare. You can expect to pay top dollar for a complete set.

UNDER WINDOW SIGNS

1939   D+ $800

38" x 12"

UNDER WINDOW SIGNS

Advertising bulletins like this were used to alert Pepsi-Cola bottlers to the availability of the latest advertising materials. These bulletins informed bottlers of everything from size to price. In many cases, they would suggest the best usage of the advertising item. The sign featured in this bulletin sold for 39 cents in 1941.

FAN PULL

1940   E $500
Fan Pull 4" x 7"

FAN PULLS

Fan pulls were fastened to the end of the fan chain to make the chain easy to grab. These pulls were also used on light cords and for decorations.

PAPER SIGNS

◄

1969   D $100
    27" x 35"

►

1950   C+ $225
Heavy Paper 20" x 28"

PEPSI & PETE

The success of the 12-ounce bottle for a nickel resulted in Pepsi-Cola becoming a major participant in consumer advertising. Almost overnight, the Pepsi-Cola Company had to develop a new and better advertising program. One of the most popular ideas  was to use a cartoon character in the Sunday funnies. The first thought was to buy Popeye the Sailor Man, and have him drink Pepsi in place of spinach. Unfortunately for Pepsi, the cost of Popeye switching from spinach to Pepsi was more than the company could afford. Pepsi management decided that they would create their own cartoon characters.

Many ideas were bounced around, from animals to children, and finally Pepsi settled on two Keystone Cop-style characters. Walter Mack, the president of the Pepsi-Cola Company at that time, decided they should be named Pepsi and Pete. So, in the fall of 1939, Pepsi and Pete made their premier appearance in magazine and newspaper ads.

From 1939 until 1951, Pepsi and Pete were featured in the comic section of the Sunday newspapers around the country. Various artists were used to draw Pepsi and Pete, including one of the most famous during that period - Rube Goldberg. The popularity of Pepsi and Pete brought about greater usage of the Pepsi-Cola cops in magazine advertising, point of purchase materials, give-away novelties, and even an animated commercial shown at movie theaters during intermission.

Today Pepsi and Pete memorabilia is at the top of the "want list" for many Pepsi collectors. Currently, Pepsi and Pete memorabilia is commanding top dollar for anything bearing the likeness of these two loveable characters.

PEPSI & PETE

1940   E $2,500

42" x 84"

PEPSI & PETE

1940   E $2,500

42" x 84"

PEPSI & PETE

1940   E $2,500
42" x 84"

PEPSI & PETE

1940   D $1,800 ▲
22" x 15"

◄
1940   D- $1,200
11" x 15"

PEPSI & PETE

1940 E+ $4,000

36" x 72"

PLAQUES

1960   B+ $45

Easel Back 11" x 9"

PLAQUES

These advertising plaques are commonly referred to as celluloids. Celluloid is a trade name for a plastic-like substance, and it is one of the components used in producing these signs. A clear plastic coating is placed on top of a round, metal disk with a cardboard backing. These can either be hung from an attached cord or as a standing display using the easel on back.

PLAQUES

◄

1954   C+ $85

Easel Back 8" x 12"

►

1954   C+ $100

Easel Back 8" x 12"

PLASTIC

1965   C $35
10" x 11"

1965   C $45
Plastic 9" x 11"

PORCELAIN SIGNS

These signs are probably the most durable and most expensive signs Pepsi ever produced. They were designed to be used in in extreme climates outdoors. For these reasons, smaller quantities of these signs were made. As a result, porcelain signs are rare and very valuable.

1940   E $350
20" x 8"

PORCELAIN SIGNS

1969   C+ $350
Die Cut18" x 42"

1950   D+ $1,200
18" x 48"

SANTAS

◄ 1951   C+ $55
20" Tall

1954   C+ $85
26" Tall   ►

THERMOMETERS

<table>
<tr><td>▲ 1945</td><td>C+</td><td>$450</td><td>1960</td><td>B</td><td>$65</td></tr>
<tr><td></td><td>16"</td><td></td><td></td><td>27"</td><td></td></tr>
</table>

◄

THERMOMETERS

◄

1965   A $15

9" x 9"

►

1971   A $10

10" x 10"

CONTAINERS

It is no accident that Containers follows Signs in this book, because the two go hand in hand. Containers, like signs, play an integral part in the marketing of Pepsi-Cola. Bottles, cans, dispensers, and vending machines all serve a dual purpose as containers and signs. In fact, even though these items were designed by engineers, the graphics and color schemes were created by advertising people. After all, getting a consumer to reach for a bottle or six-pack of Pepsi-Cola is more about attractive packaging than the structural qualities of the container.

In addition to information and prices on containers, this section offers examples of the evolution of Pepsi packaging. You can follow the changes in style and sizes of bottles from the first bottle in 1905, through the non-returnable bottles introduced in the early 1960s. In 1939, Pepsi-Cola introduced their first 6-bottle carton. Over the next 50-plus years, there have been numerous changes in both size and style of Pepsi cartons. Twelve-packs are one of the most popular forms of Pepsi packaging today. Twelve-packs were originally designed for bottles in 1947. The first Pepsi-Cola cans were cone-top shaped, so they could be filled by standard bottling equipment.

In many ways, containers and packaging mirrors the history of our time. During the great Depression, value-packaging was essential. The World War II years presented opportunities for efficient and reusable containers. The postwar years saw image and style become the dominant characteristic of Pepsi containers. In 1958, the swirl bottle was introduced. With the 1960s, came the need for convenient packaging. Cans and non-returnable bottles led the way.

THE 6-OUNCE BOTTLE ERA
1905-1933

1928

1905

1929

THE 12-OUNCE BOTTLE ERA
1934-1940

1934

1936

1939

1940

THE 12-OUNCE BOTTLE ERA
1943-1964

1951

1943

1958

THE NON-RETURNABLE BOTTLE ERA
1964-Present

Non-returnable bottles, or no deposit bottles, had been test-marketed as far back as the late 1940s. However, it wasn't until 1964 that it was decided to make non-returnables an option for Pepsi-Cola bottlers. By 1964, automobiles had made America the most mobile society in history. With this new mobility came the need for more convenient soft drink containers. Non-returnables were the perfect solution. These smaller and lighter bottles could hold as much as the larger, heavier returnables, and with no-deposit, they could be disposed of anywhere. In the past thirty years, numerous styles and shapes of non-returnable bottles have been produced. But, they lack the beauty and historical importance of the returnable bottles. Non-returnable bottles have never been as dominant as their predecessors, the returnable bottles. This is due to the popularity of the disposable aluminum cans.

PRICING

Non-returnable bottles have very limited monetary value as Pepsi collectibles. There are some exceptions. Early test market and prototype non-returnable bottles are considerably more valuable. You can expect to pay for between $1 and $5 for most non-returnables bottles.

BOTTLES

408

WHERE MANUFACTURED   YEAR

Back of bottle

DES. PAT. 12D,277

14 9 47

23 ◁◇▷ 118

Duraglas

951-G

MANUFACTURER

Bottom of bottle

This chart is for identification and dating of Pepsi bottles produced in the 1950s. The first two numbers on the back of the bottle designate the location and name of the bottle manufacturing facility. The third number corresponds with the year it was produced. In this case, the "8" is 1958. If the number does not appear on the back of the bottle, you can locate manufacturing and production dates from the codes on the bottom of the bottle.

BOTTLES

1905 ▲ E- $1,000
6 oz.

1920 C+ ▲ $150
6 oz.

BOTTLES

1940 ▲ D $125
12 oz.

1939 ▲ D $150
12 oz.

BOTTLES

1945   C+ ▲ $50
12 oz.

1940   C+ ▲ $75
12 oz.

1945   C+ ▲ $10
12 oz.

BOTTLES

1951

C+ ▲ $100

32 oz.

1947   B ▲ $5

12 oz.

1948   C ▲ $25

12 oz.

BOTTLES

1965　　C+ ▲　$45
32 oz.

1951　　D+ ▲　$150
32 oz.

1970　　B ▲　$10
32 oz.

BOTTLES

1975　　D　▲　$35
10 oz.

1976　　B　▲　$10
64 oz.

1970　　E　▲　$350
16 oz.

BOTTLES

1940   E $1,000
32 oz.   ▶

1977   ▲ C+ $50
12 oz. Special Bottle

1973   C+   ▲ $100
Anniversary Bottle 6 oz.

BOTTLES

1998　　　E　▲　$250
**Tiffany 100th
Anniversary**

1960　　　C　▲　$500
20" Tall

COMMEMORATIVE BOTTLES

The Pepsi commemorative bottle era began in the 1970s. Although there were some commemorative bottles issued prior to that time, those were mostly produced for internal awards and events, and were not widely distributed. The commemorative bottles produced from the 1970s on were produced in the hundreds of thousands. For this reason, very few of them have achieved any significant value. Most of these commemorative bottles can be purchased for between $5 and $15. This does not diminish their importance as collectibles. The events these bottles commemorate make these bottles worthy of collecting.

| 1975 | B | $6 |

16 oz.

COMMEMORATIVE BOTTLES

1975   B   ▲ $15   1975   B   ▲ $6

16 oz.   16 oz.

COMMEMORATIVE BOTTLES

1953	Tulsa, OK	$200
1971	Dallas Cowboys, TX	$20
1971	Dallas Cowboys, TX	$?
1972	Tempe, AZ	$12
1972	Orlando, FL - PCMI	$65
1973	Greenville, SC	$12
1973	New Bern, NC (Tall)	$75
1973	New Bern, NC (Short)	$75
1973	Owen, IL Plaque/Bot.	$75
1973	Owen, IL Bottle Only	$50
1974	St. Louis, MO (Proto)	$100
1974	St. Louis, MO	$12
1974	Nebraska Cornhuskers	$12
1974	Clemson University	$12
1974	Anderson, IN	$12
1974	Columbia, SC	$?
1974	Greenville, SC	$12
1974	Spartanburg, SC	$?
1975	Greenville, SC	$12
1975	Johnson, TN ETSU	$12
1975	Cincinnati, OH	$12
1975	Cincy., OH (No Red)	$20
1975	Tampa, FL (Small)	$12
1975	Tampa, FL (Large)	$25
1975	Pennsauken, NJ Drum	$?
1975	Cheverly, MD Drum	$8
1975	Pennsauken, NJ Eagles	$?
1975	Cheverly, MD Eagle	$8
1975	Pennsauken, NJ Flag	$?
1975	Cheverly, MD Flag	$8
1975	Pennsauken, NJ Wash.	$?
1975	Cheverly, MD Wash.	$8
1975	Pennsauken, NJ (York)	$?
1975	Cheverly, MD (York)	$8
1976	Original 1 Liter Gold	$75
1976	Tar Heels, NC (10 Oz.)	$12

COMMEMORATIVE BOTTLES

1976	Tar Heels, NC (16 Oz.)	$12
1976	Gadsen, AL	$12
1976	KY Bicentennial	$12
1976	KY Bicent. Prototype	$100
1976	Tucson, AZ	$12
1976	Denver, CO Bicent.	$12
1976	Denver, CO Bicent.	$20
1976	Macon, GA	$12
1976	Greenville, SC	$12
1976	#1 Old Dominion - VA	$25
1976	#1 Old Dominion - VA	$12
1976	#2 Famous Statesman	$12
1976	St. Louis Arch Proto.	$125
1976	New Bern, NC	$12
1976	Miami, OH Erie Canal	$12
1976	Ft. Amanda/Finley, OH	$12
1976	Ohio - Appleseed	$50
1976	Ohio - Appleseed	$12
1976	Anderson, SC	$12
1976	Fort Wayne, IN	$125
1976	Mtn. State - WV	$12
1976	Famous Places - WV	$12
1977	Safford, AZ	$12
1977	Iowa Vs. Iowa State	$12
1977	OK City, OK	$75
1978	Iowa Vs. Iowa State	$12
1978	Iowa Vs. ISU (Green)	$12
1978	Vancouver, B.C.	$40
1979	Greenville, NC (Dew)	$30
1979	Bennettsville, SC	$60
1979	Memphis, MO	$100
1980	Charlotte, NC	$12
1980	Anderson, SC	$12
1980	Bennettsville, SC	$12
1980	Charleston, SC	$12
1980	Columbia, SC	$12

COMMEMORATIVE BOTTLES

1980	Conway, SC	$12
1980	Florence, SC	$12
1980	Greenville, SC	$12
1980	Spartanburg, SC	$12
1980	Rio Piedras, P.R.	$10
1980	Rio Piedras, P.R.	$10
1981	Marshall Vs. Army	$25
1982	Bainbridge, GA	$40
1982	Tulsa, OK	$15
1983	Saluki Pride, IL	$12
1983	Saluki Pride (Green)	$?
1983	Fresno, CA	$12
1983	Connersville, IN	$12
1983	Charlottesville 75	$15
1983	Cincinnati, OH	$100
1984	UI Rose Bowl	$20
1984	Missouri St. Univ.	$12
1984	Winston/Salem, NC	$25
1984	Jackson, MS	$100
1984	Jackson, MS (No Red)	$125
1984	Portsmouth, OH	$75
1986	Mt. Vernon, OH	$40
1986	NC 50th Anniversary	$60
1986	Tenn. Homecoming	$15
1986	Denver, CO 50th Ann.	$30
1986	Moultrie, GA	$15
1988	Nashville, TN	$25
1988	Charlotte, NC	$12
1988	Moultrie, GA	$15
1990	Dollywood, TN	$15
1990	Philadelphia, PA	$15
1990	Philadelphia, PA -Diet	$20
1990	Batavia, NY	$20
1990	Ray Charles	$?
1991	Columbia, SC - Petty	$6
1991	Columbia, SC 7 Time	$6

COMMEMORATIVE BOTTLES

1991	Columbia, SC 200 Wn.	$6
1991	100th Nascar Start	$6
1991	Bakersfield, CA	$8
1991	Dollywood, TN	$12
1991	Dollywood, TN	$15
1991	Georgia So. Eagles	$15
1991	Bainbridge, GA	$15
1991	Wenatchee, WA	$60
1991	1st Winston Cup Race	$4
1991	Most. Conseq. Wins	$4
1991	Most Wins in Season	$4
1991	Most Poles in Career	$4
1991	Most Popular Driver	$4
1991	200 Career Victories	$4
1991	1st Winston Cup Vict.	$4
1991	Petty's Final Year	$4
1992	1987 Stars & Stripes	$6
1992	1988 Stars & Stripes	$6
1992	1992 Stars & Stripes	$12
1993	Houston, TX	$8
1993	Knoxville, IA	$8
1993	Vancouver, BC	$15
1993	Vancouver, BC	$15
1993	Shaq - Chillin	$4
1993	Shaq - Stuffin	$4
1993	Shaq -Scorin	$4
1993	Shaq - Spinnin	$4
1993	Shaq - Slammin	$4
1993	Shaq - Jammin	$4
1994	Albq. Air Balloon	$8
1994	San Jose Sharks	$8
1994	Spartansburg, SC	$8
1994	Kissimmee, FL	$12
1995	Modesto, CA	$8
1995	Kissimmee, FL	$8

COMMEMORATIVE BOTTLES

1991   E $500
Silver Dipped Petty
Set

1992   C $35
America's Cup Set

COMMEMORATIVE BOTTLES

▲ 1998   B $25
100th Anniversary
4 Pack

▲ 1996   B+ $10
AZ Diamondbacks
4 Pack

LABELS

1905   E $800

LABELS

These are the most common labels used by the Pepsi-Cola Company in the last 100 years. There were many other labels produced bearing minor differences, such as the addition of the name of the franchise where the Pepsi was bottled.

Finding an intact label is a rare occurrence. Most of these labels were destroyed during use. There are a number of reproduction labels being sold as authentic by unscrupulous dealers.

LABELS

▲ 1939　　D　　$75

▲ 1941　　C　　$25

CANS

1969   E $150
12 oz.

1950   C+ $300
Cone Top 12 oz.

CANS

◄ 1973   B+ $10
12 oz.

1979   A   ► $5
16.9 oz.

COMMEMORATIVE & CONTEST CANS

1988   A $2
12 oz.

COMMEMORATIVE & CONTEST CANS

Over the last 30 years, Pepsi-Cola has produced hundreds of millions of commemorative cans. They have also produced almost as many to promote contests. One example is the Jackson's Victory Tour can. This can was distributed nationwide, with over 50 million produced. Consequently, almost every collector has a Jackson Victory Tour can and, as a result, there is very little monetary value to this can.

Collecting commemorative cans is quite popular, due to the low cost and availability of the cans. One thing to keep in mind while collecting cans is that they must be drained. Any soft drink stored over a period of time will eventually begin to leak. It is recommended that you carefully poke holes in the bottom of cans and drain, rather than opening and draining from the top. Most can collectors feel this is an acceptable way to preserve the value of the can.

COMMEMORATIVE & CONTEST CANS

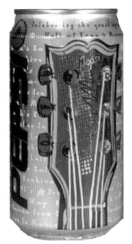

▲ 1995   A $2
12 oz.

▲ 1976   A $2
12 oz.

COMMEMORATIVE & CONTEST CANS

◄

1999   D $100
Destiny Can

►

1991   D $25
6" x 4" x 4"

MULTI-PACK CANS

▲ 1965   D $50
6 Pack

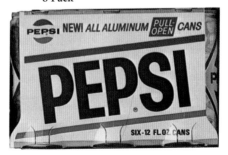

▲ 1965   C $200
12" x 10"

MULTI-PACK CANS

▲ 1950   E $300
Cardboard Box

▲ 1973   C+ $35
6 Pack

COMMEMORATIVE & CONTEST CANS

▲ 1999   D+ $100
11" x 6" x 3"

◄

1994   C+ $45
36" Tall

MULTI-BOTTLE PACKAGING

MULTI-BOTTLE PACKAGING

Multi-bottle packaging has become commonplace over the last 50 years. It is hard to imagine that this wasn't always the situation. Original Pepsi-Cola in bottles was sold primarily as a single drink. It wasn't until 1939 that Pepsi-Cola was sold and marketed in a 6-bottle carton. This was a result of the increased availability of ice boxes and electric refrigerators. At this time, a single 12-ounce bottle of Pepsi-Cola sold for a nickel, or a 6-bottle carton for 25 cents. This was the beginning of what has become known as the "take-home" market. From 1939 to the present, multi-bottle and can packaging has mushroomed. The multi-container packaging has consisted of 2-packs, 4-packs, 6-packs, 8-packs, 12-packs, and 24-packs. The material used for packaging Pepsi bottles and cans has included paper, cardboard, cloth, metal, wood, and plastic. As the public's thirst has increased, so has the need for more convenient ways to get Pepsi home to the consumers.

MULTI-BOTTLE PACKAGING

▲ 1940   D $75
6 Bottles

▲ 1940   D $75
6 Bottles

MULTI-BOTTLE PACKAGING

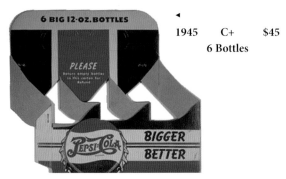

1945   C+ $45
6 Bottles

▲ 1951   C+ $35
12 Bottles

MULTI-BOTTLE PACKAGING

▲ 1954   C $20
12 Bottles

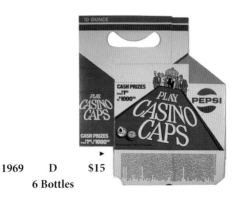

1969   D $15
6 Bottles

CLOTH CARRIERS

1943   C+ $65
Cloth 6 Bottles

PAPER CARRIERS

During the late 1930s and early 1940s, these paper bag carriers were quite popular. They were basically disposable Pepsi carriers. Due to the weight of the bottles, these carriers did not last more than a few trips.

During World War II, the use of paper carriers was necessary due to material shortages.

PAPER CARRIERS

◄

1939   E $100
    Paper 6 Bottles

1940   C+ $75   ►
    Paper 6 Bottles

PAPER CARRIERS

1945   C+ $75
Paper 6 Bottles

1940   D $75
Paper 6 Bottles

CARDBOARD CARRIERS

1945   D $100 ▲
Cardboard 24 Bottles

▲ 1950   C+ $75
Cardboard 24 Bottles

WOOD CARRIERS

1940   E $225
    Masonite 6 Bottles

1940   C+ $175
    Wood 6 Bottles

WOOD CARRIERS

▲ 1940   C+ $65
Wood 24 Bottles

▲ 1940   C+ $65
Wood 24 Bottles

METAL CARRIERS

1940   D $150
Metal 12 Bottles

1940   D $125
Metal 6 Bottles

CARRIERS

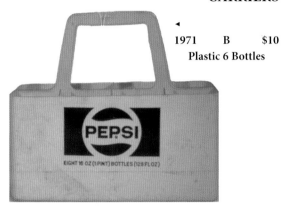

◄

1971   B $10

Plastic 6 Bottles

▲ **1940   C+ $60**

Metal 24 Bottle

PICNIC COOLERS

1965   C+ $35

13" Tall

This picnic cooler was originally art on the cover of a Pepsi World magazine. After the bottlers received their magazines, they requested that Pepsi actually produce this picnic cooler. In 1965, it was made available to Pepsi bottlers and the public.

PICNIC COOLERS

◄
1969　　B+　　$20
　　　13" Tall

1965　　C　　$50
　　　13" Tall

PICNIC COOLERS

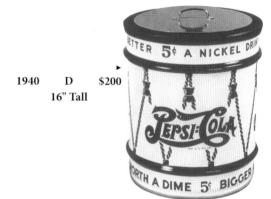

1940   D $200
16" Tall

1954   B+ $20
9" Tall

PICNIC COOLERS

◄
1951   C $100
18" x 18"

1945   D $200
14" x 12"   ►

ICE COOLERS

1940   D $800
27" x 15"

ICE COOLERS

Before the invention of electric refrigeration, stores that sold cold bottles of Pepsi-Cola relied on these types of ice coolers. The major drawback to this type of cooler was the constant need to replace the ice.

ICE COOLERS

◄ 1934   D+ $1,200
        31" x 33"

1934   E $1,500
        31" x 33"

ELECTRIC COOLERS

1945   C+ $600
44" x 35"

ELECTRIC COOLERS

In 1940, Pepsi began using electric coolers. These new coolers worked by circulating cold water through the internal container. These coolers were notorious for causing the paper labels to come off the bottles. Eventually these water coolers were replaced by air coolers.

Most chest coolers, or flat-top coolers, were also available as vendors. The vendors had a rack inside that held the bottles by the neck. After placing money into the coin mechanism, the bottle slid along this rack to an opening activated by the coin drop.

ELECTRIC COOLERS

◄ 1940   D+ $1,500
34" x 45"

◄
1941   E $800
44" x 35"

ELECTRIC VENDOR

1951   D $2,000

24" x 52"

Vendolator 27B

ELECTRIC VENDOR

1955   C $500

47" x 33"

Bevco 160

ELECTRIC CUP VENDOR

1955   D+ $400

28" x 70"

Premix Vendor

ELECTRIC COOLERS

1955　　D　　$500

39" x 72"

United Visi-Cooler

P384

CROWNS

1905   E $75

First Crown

CROWNS

Crowns, or bottle caps, have been used by the Pepsi-Cola Company since 1905. At first, they were simply used to seal and mark the bottles. Later on, they became an important part of the promotion of Pepsi-Cola. As early as 1910, crowns were used as tokens to exchange for merchandise. The success of this program spawned other crown redemption programs over the years.

Crowns were also used as pieces in various Pepsi contests. Specially marked crowns were placed on random bottles of Pepsi with prizes or money designated underneath the cork. Many collectors of crowns specialize in collecting these contest bottle caps.

CROWNS

▲ 1936   C- $10

▲ 1939   D $20
Promotional Crown

▲ 1941   C $10

▲ 1941   D $20
Promotional Crown

CROWNS

1951   B   ▲ $5

1991   A   ▲ $1

1965   A   ▲ $2

1971   A   ▲ $1

CROWNS

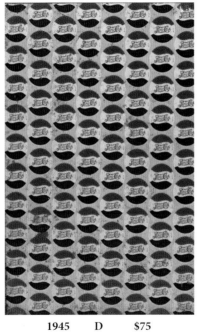

1945   D $75

Uncut Crowns

PAPER CUP HOLDERS

1954   B+ $30

Paper 6 Cup Holder

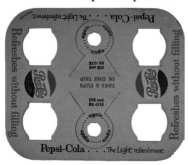

CUPS

1940   E $65
12 oz.

1940   D+ $50
10 oz.

CUPS

1964   B $5
10 oz.

1960   B $5
10 oz.

CUPS

◄ 1969   B $3
    10 oz.

1979   A $1
    16 oz.

FOLDING PAPER CUP

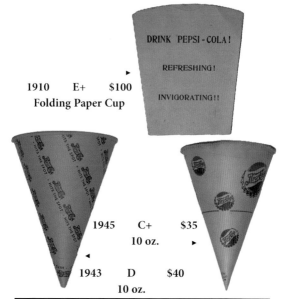

1910   E+ $100
Folding Paper Cup

DRINK PEPSI - COLA!

REFRESHING!

INVIGORATING!!

1945   C+ $35
10 oz.

1943   D $40
10 oz.

FOLDING PAPER CUP

The cup on the left, is the rarest of all Pepsi cups. Unfortunately, the graphics are quite plain, which inhibits the collector value of this item.

FOLDING PAPER CUP

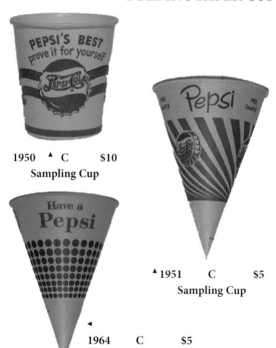

1950 ▲ C $10
Sampling Cup

▲ 1951 C $5
Sampling Cup

◄ 1964 C $5
10 oz.

FOUNTAIN DISPENSERS

1905   E+ $15,000
Ceramic 18" Tall

1905 DISPENSER

The dispenser on the left is an original Pepsi dispenser used in soda fountains in the early 1900s. Because of the fragile nature of ceramic, not many survive. They are very rare and sought after by collectors. There is no Pepsi collectible coveted more than the original syrup dispenser.

The dispenser above was reissued by the Pepsi-Cola Company. It is a limited edition of only 300.

FOUNTAIN DISPENSERS

1983   D+ $2,000
Ceramic 18" tall

FOUNTAIN DISPENSERS

1945 ▲ D	$800	1945 ▲ D+	$1,000
20" Tall		20" Tall	

FOUNTAIN DISPENSERS

▲ 1949　　C　　$225
Musical 6" tall

1954　▲　D-　　$350
20" tall

FOUNTAIN DISPENSERS

In 1934, Pepsi-Cola was reborn with the introduction of the 12-ounce bottle for 5 cents. The success of the 12-ounce bottle caused Pepsi to all but abandon the fountain business. In 1943, it was decided that Pepsi could no longer ignore this important part of the soft drink business. The company's timing could not have been worse. World War II was at its peak. There were severe material shortages, which made it impossible for Pepsi to get a regular supply of modern fountain dispensers. They were forced to re-enter the fountain business with antiquated equipment. For this reason, Pepsi had to resort to the use of hand-operated equipment to dispense Pepsi-Cola at fountains.

Following the war, Pepsi introduced modern fountain equipment to their customers. From 1945 on, Pepsi used fountain equipment that automatically mixed syrup and carbonated water.

1951   C+ $200

FOUNTAIN DISPENSERS

◄

1943   D $500

►

1960   C+ $250

FOUNTAIN DISPENSERS

1960   D $300
24" tall

1965   D $150
Home Dispenser

FOUNTAIN DRINKING GLASSES

Fountain drinking glasses, decorated with the Pepsi-Cola logo, have been around since 1905. The earliest Pepsi drinking glasses sell for around $1000, and are very hard to find. It wasn't until the 1940s that fountain drinking glasses were issued on a regular basis.

1949 ▲ **C+** $45
10 oz.

1943 ▲ **B+** $20
10 oz.

PROMOTIONAL DRINKING GLASSES

Promotional drinking glasses, or glasses that are to be given away or sold at a reduced price, have been around since the early 1940s. These were designed to enhance the sale of Pepsi-Cola. The first known promotional glass is the Pepsi & Pete glass. These glasses are in great demand by Pepsi collectors. Regretfully, these glasses have been reproduced. A quick way to recognize the reproduction is that they were manufactured by Anchor-Hocking. The original glass was produced by Owens-Illinois.

1940   D $400

10 oz.

PROMOTIONAL DRINKING GLASSES

1965　　B+　　$20

New Haven, MO

1965　　C+　　$25

Wichita Falls, TX

1967　　C+　　$25

Ft. Smith, AR

1980　　B　　$20

Eau Claire, WI

PROMOTIONAL DRINKING GLASSES

1969   D $30

Bottler's Convention

1965   D $35

Sales Meeting

1975   D $30

Bottler's Association

1976   D $30

Bottler's Association

PROMOTIONAL DRINKING GLASSES

1995   E $200

Large Display Glass

1980   A $1

16 oz.

1990   A+ $3

With lid 12 oz.

1980   A $10

Set of 4 in box

PROMOTIONAL DRINKING GLASSES

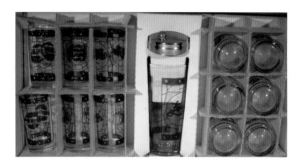

1973   C+ $150
75th Anniversary Set

CARTOON GLASSES

Most cartoon glasses are fairly common and are priced below $10 each. There are a few exceptions that are quite valuable and rare. There were millions of these glasses produced during the 1970s. The following is a list of the more common glasses.

PEPSI COLLECTOR SERIES 1973 WARNER BROS.

Beaky Buzzard
Bugs Bunny
Cool Cat
Daffy Duck
Elmer Fudd
Foghorn Leghorn
Henery Hawk
Pepe LePew
Petunia Pig
Porky Pig
Road Runner
Slow Poke Rodriguez
Sylvester
Speedy Gonzales
Tasmanian Devil
Tweety
Wile E. Coyote
Yosemite Sam

PEPSI COLLECTOR SERIES 1976 WARNER BROS. ACTION

Beaky/Cool Cat/Kite
Bugs/Mirror/Ray Gun/Martian
Cool Cat/Coconut/Hunter
Daffy/Elmer/Bugs/Sign
Daffy/Tasmanian Devil/Fire Cracker
Elmer/Bugs/Gun/Carrots
Foghorn/Dog/Dog House/Bomb
Hoppy/Sylvester Jr./Sylvester Boxing
Pepe/Cat/Perfume
Pepe/Hose/Daffy/Kink
Petunia/Painting/Porky/Mowing
Porky/Fishing/Tasmanian Devil/
    Fish
Porky/Pot/Daffy/Ladle
Road Runner/Catapult/Coyote/Rock
Slow Poke/Speedy/Sylvester/
    Hammer
Sylvester/Granny/Tweety/Birdbath
Sylvester/Limb/Tweety/Sawing
Sylvester/Tweety/Net/Bulldog
Wile/Sheep/Sheepdog/Rope
Wile/Skateboard & Sail/Road
    Runner
Yosemite/Goldpan/Speedy/Gold
Yosemite/Pirate/Bugs/Cannon

PEPSI SYRUP

1905   E+ $2,000

12"

PEPSI SYRUP

Pepsi-Cola is made by combining carbonated water and Pepsi syrup. This was done at the bottling plant on a large scale, and at the local soda fountain for a single serving. One ounce of Pepsi syrup was combined with five ounces of carbonated water to produce a glass of Pepsi-Cola.

PEPSI SYRUP

1909   D+ ▲ $100
1 gallon

1945   C+ ▲ $125
1 gallon

PEPSI SYRUP

1954   C $45
1 gallon

1960   B+ $30
1 gallon

PEPSI CONCENTRATE

1945   D+ $225

5 gallons

PEPSI CONCENTRATE

Pepsi concentrate is all the ingredients that make Pepsi-Cola syrup, with the exception of water and sugar. Pepsi bottlers buy concentrate from the Pepsi-Cola Company, then mix it with water and sugar to produce Pepsi-Cola syrup. From there, the syrup is either used to bottle Pepsi or sold to fountains that dispense Pepsi.

In the 1930s, Pepsi-Cola concentrate sold for $350 for a 10 gallon barrel like those pictured.

PEPSI CONCENTRATE

1960   C+ $35

    Holds 4 syrup jugs

◄

        1939   D $175

           10 gallons

PEPSI CONCENTRATE

◄ 1940   E $200
        10 gallons

1940   C+ $125
     10 gallons

PEPSI CONCENTRATE

1947   C+ $150
10 gallons

1940   C+ $125
10 gallons

PEPSI CONCENTRATE

| 1939 | E | $350 |

10 gallons

A kit was available to convert these barrels into ice coolers.

NOVELTIES, TOYS & ACCESSORIES

Novelties, toys, and accessories is the broadest category in this book. It pretty much covers everything that doesn't fit in any of the other sections.

Novelties are relatively inexpensive items that are given away to promote brand recognition and goodwill. Novelty items were commonly given away at plant openings and special events. Some of the more common novelties given away over the years have been pencils, pens, cigarette lighters, ashtrays, and keychains. Items such as cigarette lighters and ashtrays are especially interesting today, in light of the growing trend against smoking—it is unlikely that novelties associated with smoking will be made in the future. Miniature bottles are among the most popular novelties produced. For the most part, they were distributed between 1940 and 1980. Many collectors favor these miniatures because of their detail and realistic appearance. Salt and pepper shakers have been popular novelties for over fifty years. Some may think that these should be fountain items, because they were used in restaurants and other places that served Pepsi. While this is true, the vast majority of salt and pepper shakers were distributed to the public as novelties.

Toys bearing the Pepsi-Cola logos have been produced as far back as the 1930s. In this category, there are two types of toys. The first is toys that were produced for the Pepsi-Cola Company as promotional items. These types of toys are usually the less valuable of the Pepsi toys. One example is the Pepsi bank in the shape of a Pepsi cooler. These were made for the Pepsi-Cola Company, who in turn offered them to their customers for resale to the public. The second type of toys are those licensed by Pepsi-Cola to be manufactured and sold by toy companies. These toys are generally made to a higher standard.

Accessories include an assortment of Pepsi items that bear the Pepsi trademark, and range from ties to umbrellas. Many of these accessories were produced for the Pepsi-Cola Company to use in everyday operations, such as embroidered emblems. Other accessories, such as umbrellas, were used as gifts for customers.

AWARDS

1956　　C　　$35
18" x 12"

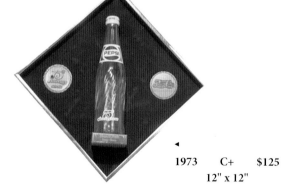

1973　　C+　　$125
12" x 12"

AWARDS

1965   C $75
18" x 20"

AWARDS

1960   C+ $45
    4" x 4"

▲ 1981   B+ $20
    25" x 15"

CALENDARS

▲ 1909   D+ $2,500
10" x 18"

▲ 1921   E $1,500
14" x 20"

CALENDARS

1941   D+ $300
29" x 43"

1940   D $200
15" x 23"

CALENDARS

◄

1948   D+ $350
    6" x 8"

1956   D- $150
    8" x 12"

►

CALENDARS

1964   C $45

      8" x 12"

▲ 1970   C $45

     20" x 10"

CALENDARS

1969   C $45 ▲
20" x 10"

►
1946   B $35
15" x 20"

EMBROIDERED EMBLEMS

Embroidered emblems, also known as patches, were initially used as markings for Pepsi employees and route salesmen. Most of the emblems in this section are that type. In later years, embroidered emblems were produced as souvenirs for Pepsi sponsored events and other special promotions. Today there are very few of these produced, which makes the older emblems more interesting and collectible.

1940   D+ $45
10"

EMBROIDERED EMBLEMS

◄ 1951   C $25
        7"

▲ 1971   A $5
        9"

EMBROIDERED EMBLEMS

1954   C $20
7"

1940   C+ $20
2"

EMBROIDERED EMBLEMS

◄
1963   C $15
7"

▲ 1940   C+ $20
3"

EMBROIDERED EMBLEMS

1963   C   ▶ $5

         3"

    ▲ 1964   A+ $5

         3"

EMBROIDERED EMBLEMS

▲ 1978   A $5
       4"

▲ 1982   A $5
       4"

FANS

Fans have been a useful advertising novelty distributed by the Pepsi-Cola Company since the early 1900s. In the days before air conditioning, fans were a necessity, especially in public places. Fans were used in movie theaters, churches, restaurants, baseball games and various other community gatherings.

The earliest fans were made of a thin paper-like material that resulted in most of them being lost due to deterioration.

1906   E+ $1,800
Paper (Reverse)

FANS

1949   D $125
Cardboard (Front)
10" tall

Reverse

FANS

1940   C $125
Cardboard (Front)
11" tall

FOUNTAIN

◄ 1909   E+ $8,000
Strawholder 6" tall

1909   E+ $250 ►
Strawholder 5" x 4"

FOUNTAIN

1945   E $1,200
7" x 11"

1940   D+ $200
Toothpick Holder

FOUNTAIN

◄

1962   C $35
Toothpick Holder

1978   B $15
Napkin Holder

FOUNTAIN

1945   D $600
Napkin Holder 7" x 5"

If you sold Pepsi-Cola at your soda fountain or restaurant during the 1940s, these are the types of promotional items the Pepsi-Cola Company might have given you to use in your establishment.

FOUNTAIN

◄
1945   D $45
Dispenser Handle

►
1960   C $10
Dispenser Handle

FOUNTAIN

1960   C $15

Dispenser Handle

1964   C+ $20

Dispenser Handle

FOUNTAIN

◄
1960   C $10
Dispenser Handle

►
1987   B $5
Dispenser Handle

FOUNTAIN

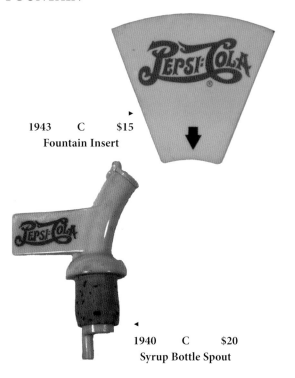

1943   C $15
Fountain Insert

1940   C $20
Syrup Bottle Spout

KEYCHAINS

◄
1945   B $10
Resealable Cap

1940 ▲ D $55
Keychain/Coin Saver

1951   D ▲ $75
Keychain/Flashlight

KEYCHAINS

1951 ▲ C $15
Keychain

▲1951 C+ $25
Keychain

1954 ▶ D $25
Two View Keychain

KEYCHAINS

◄

1951   C $10
Keychain

1951   C+ $20
Keychain

▶

KEYCHAINS

1970 ▲ B	$5	1962 ▲ B	$5
Keychain		Keychain	

KEYCHAINS

◄ 1962   B $5
Keychain

1943 ▲ D $85
Lapel Pin

◄
1960   C $25
Lapel Pin

LAPEL PIN

1910 ▲ D+ $250
Lapel Pin

1910 ▲ E $550
Service Pin

1943 ▲ D+ $75
Service Pin

1943 ▲ D+ $75
Service Pin

LAPEL PIN

1945   D+ $75
◄   Service Pin

1951 ▲ D $75
Safety Award Pin

◄
1953   C+ $65
Service Pin

LAPEL PIN

1951   E $65
Service Pin

1955   D $60
Service Pin

LAPEL PIN

1970 ▲ C $25
Service Pin

1991 ▲ C $25
Charm

◄
1991 C $35
Service Pin

MINIATURES

1940 ▲ D+ $125

Salt & Pepper

1940 ▲ D $150

Salt & Pepper

1940 ▲ D $175

Salt & Pepper

1941 ▲ C+ $150

Salt & Pepper

NOVELTIES

▲ 1985   B $15

Digital Clock

▲ 1967   C $25

License Plate

NOVELTIES

◄ 1980   A $35
Telephone

▲ 1978   C+ $100
Telephone

◄ 1970   B $5
Flashlight

NOVELTIES

▲ 1940   D $45
Wallet

▲ 1975   B $5
Belt Buckle

NOVELTIES

▲ 1940   D $150
Glass Slide

▲ 1985   D $100
Cell 10" x 8"

NOVELTIES

▲ 1910   E $600

Desk Set

▲ 1940   D+ $400

Pencil Holder

NOVELTIES

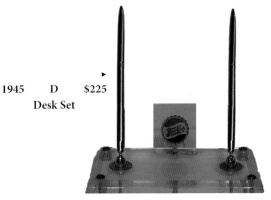

1945   D $225
Desk Set

1940   D+ $650
Desk Set

NOVELTIES

◄
1960   C $50
Paper Weight

1995   A $35
Commemorative

NOVELTIES

1981   C+ $30
Can in Lucite 6" x 4"

1975   D $45
Convention
Commemorative

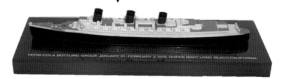

NOVELTIES

◄ 1990   D $35
Gift Item

1939   D- $100
Mystery Knife

►

NOVELTIES

1960   C+ $25
Novelty Crown

1959   C+ $45
Novelty Crown

1909   E $250
Shoeshine Brush

NOVELTIES

1958   B $20
Novelty Crown

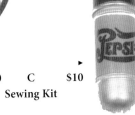

1950   C $10
Sewing Kit

1940   D $45
Sewing Kit

NOVELTIES

1967   C+ $45
Change Plate

1967   C+ $45
Change Plate

NOVELTIES

◄

1968   C+ $45
Change Plate

▲1970   B+ $10
Grocery Divider

NOVELTIES

1960   C+ $35
Change Mat

▲1975   B+ $10
Grocery Divider

NOVELTIES

◄ 1965   C $25

Change Mat

▲ 1975   C $50

Door Mat

OPENERS

1940   D $85
Wall Mount

New   A $10
Wall Mount

OPENERS

1943 ▲ D $45
Plastic Handle

1940 ▲ D- $45
Plastic Handle

1920 D $85
Metal

OPENERS

1960   B $2
Metal/Plastic

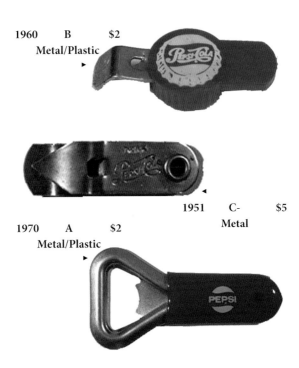

1951   C- $5
Metal

1970   A $2
Metal/Plastic

PENCILS

1920 ▲ D $25
Pencil Clip

1951 ▲ B $2
Pencil Clip

1945 ▲ B+ $10
Pencil Clip

1951 ▲ B $2
Pencil Clip

PENCILS

1960   B $3

1979   A $1

1940   C+ $55

1940   C+ $55

PENS

1951   C+ $25

1940   C+ $60

1940   D $75

PENS

1951   B+ $15

1940   C+ $125

Fountain

1951   B+ $5

PENS

1980   A $1

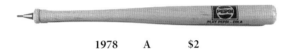

1978   A $2

1951   D $45
Fountain

PINBACK BUTTONS

1940   E $400

1909   E+ $1,200

PINBACK BUTTONS

1910   E+ $600

1940   D $45

1940   C+ $35

PINBACK BUTTONS

1945   C+ $25

1940   D $35

1943   E $75

PINBACK BUTTONS

1947   C $25

1950   D $30

1951   D $40

1951   B $10

PINBACK BUTTONS

1951 ▲   B $10

1956   D $65 ▲

◄

1956   C $35

PINBACK BUTTONS

| 1956 | C | $20 | | 1958 | C | $15 |

| 1959 | B | $5 | | 1959 | C | $5 |

PINBACK BUTTONS

1960   C+ $30

1962   C+ $25

1956   C $15

1960   C $15

PINBACK BUTTONS

1964   B $10

1964   B $10

1968   C $10

1965   C+ $10

PINBACK BUTTONS

1964   C $10   1965   C $10

1967   B $5   1972   C $5

PINBACK BUTTONS

1969   C $10

1976   B $5

1976   B $3

1978   A $2

PINBACK BUTTONS

1980   C $10

1978   C $5

1980   A $2

1956   C+ $10

PINBACK BUTTONS

1978   A $2

1979   A $2

1964   C $10

1990   C $5

PINBACK BUTTONS

1976   B $3

1978   A $2

1956   D $40

1964   D $40

CONVENTION PINBACK BUTTONS

During the 1950s and early 1960s, Pepsi was engaged in promoting its soft drink at various national events. Free samples of Pepsi-Cola were dispensed at the Republican and Democratic National Conventions. In addition, pinback buttons were given out that featured political themes and Pepsi-Cola. At the Republican Conventions, buttons with elephants were given out. At the Democratic Convention, donkeys were imprinted on the buttons. This program was conducted from 1956 through 1964.

1956   D   ▲ $40

1956   D   ▲ $40

CONVENTION PINBACK BUTTONS

| 1956 | D | $40 | 1960 | D | $40 |

| 1956 | D | $40 | 1964 | D | $40 |

CONVENTION PINBACK BUTTONS

1964   C+ $25

1964   D $40

PLAYING CARDS

1942   D $65

1945   D $75

PLAYING CARDS

◄ 1940   D $45

1961   C+ $20 ►

PLAYING CARDS

◄ 1951   C+ $40

1964   C+ $20 ►

PLAYING CARDS

1958   D $85   ▲

▶

1971   C+ $15

PLAYING CARDS

1964   C+ $20

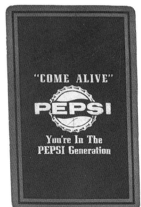

1983   ▲ A $10

1987   A $5

PLAYING CARDS

1976　　C+　▲　$95　　　　1976　　C+　▲　$95

1983　　B　▲　$10

PLAYING CARDS

1976 ▲ C+ $95

1980 ▲ A $5

1980 ▲ B $10

PLAYING CARDS

1983 ▲ A $5

1980 ▲ A $5

1958   D $175
Double Set

RADIOS

◄ 1947   C+ $120
Tube/Bakelite

1964   C+ ▲ $125
Transistor

◄ 1955   D+ $1,100
Tube

RADIOS

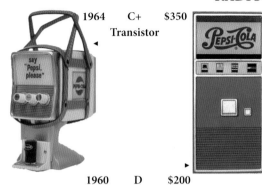

1964   C+ $350
Transistor

1960   D $200
Transistor

▲ 1967   D $500
AM/FM

RADIOS

1983　　B　　$15
AM/Headphones

1970　　A　　$15
Transistor

1980　　B　　$35
Transistor

RADIOS

1987   C $35

Transistor

1981   ▲ C $45

Transistor

1978   A $15

Transistor

RECORDS

1943   C+ $55

With Envelope

1943   C+ $20

With Envelope

1943   C $20

With Envelope

Envelope

RECORDS

▲ 1969   C+ $10
Promotional

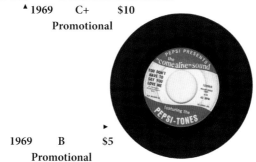

1969   B   ▶ $5
Promotional

RECORDS

▲ 1961   B $5
Promotional

◄ 1980   A $5
Promotional

RECORDS

1978 ▲ A $3
Promotional

1971 C+ $5
Convention Gift

RECORDS

▲ 1965   B $10
Promotional

◄

1965   B $10
Radio Ads

RECORDS

1970   B $10 ▲
Radio Ads

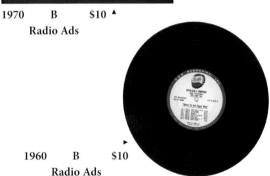

1960   B $10
Radio Ads

RECORDS

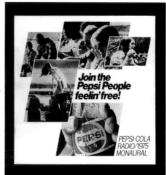

1975   B $10
   Radio Ads

1977   B+ $10
   Radio Ads

RECORDS

◄ 1976   B $10
      Radio Ads

1977   B $10   ►
    Radio Ads

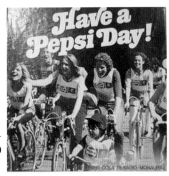

RECORDS

1986   C $15
Convention Gift

RULERS

1951   C $10
Metal

1960   C+ $10
Metal

1961   C $10
Metal

ASHTRAYS

1945   C+ $100
3" x 3"

1940   C+ $150
3" x 3"

1945   C+ $75
4" dia.

ASHTRAYS

1945   C+ $100
5" x 5"

1958   D+ $100
6" x 6"

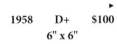

1961   D+ $125
6" dia.

ASHTRAYS

1966   C $25
4" dia.

1960   C $50
4" x 4"

1951   C $15
4" x 4"

ASHTRAYS

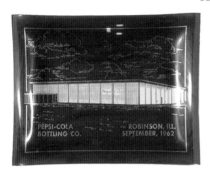

1962   C+   ▲ $40
      5" x 7"

1965   ▲ C+ $45
Plant Opening

ASHTRAYS

▲ 1969   C $15
3" x 3"

◄
1951   C $25
3" dia.

ASHTRAYS

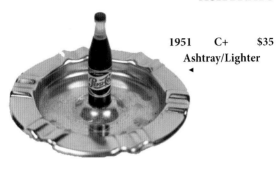

1951 C+ $35
Ashtray/Lighter
◄

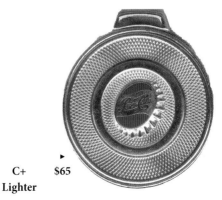

►
1960 C+ $65
Lighter

LIGHTERS

1945 ▲ C $60

Lighter

1960 ▲ B+ $25

Lighter

▲

1940   C+ $45

Cigarette Holder

LIGHTERS

◄

1964   A $10
     Lighter

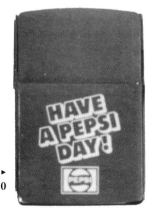

1976   A $10
     Lighter

►

LIGHTERS

1960　　D　　$75

1954　　D　　$75

1954　　D-　　$75

1951　　D-　　$75

LIGHTERS

1964	D-	$75	1960	B	$15
1954	B+	$30	1964	B+	$30

LIGHTERS

1964　　B+　　$30　　　　1964　　B+　　$30

1965　　A　　$10　　　　1960　　A　　$10

LIGHTERS

1965   C+ $15

1960   A $5

1951   A $20

1980   A $10

LIGHTERS

1956   C $45

1951   D $150
Musical

LIGHTERS

1951   C+ $125
Musical

◄

►

1961   D $150
Musical

MATCHBOOKS

1940   D+ $50

1910   E+ $175

MATCHBOOKS

◄ 1939   D- $40

► 1939   D- $40

MATCHBOOKS

1937   C+ $10

1939   C+ $15

MATCHBOOKS

1940   C $5

1940   C+ $10

MATCHBOOKS

1940   C+ $10

1940   C $10

MATCHBOOKS

1940   C- $5

1945   E- $5

MATCHBOOKS

1950	C+	$25

1950   C+ $25

1950   C+ $25

1950   C $5

MATCHBOOKS

▲ 1950   C+ $2 5

1976   A $2

◄ 1951   C+ $10

MATCHBOOKS

1951   D $20

1962   ▲ B $3

1960   B $5

DISNEY MATCHBOOKS

Disney and Pepsi-Cola are two of the most collectible trademarks in existence. Combine them and you usually end up with something very special. That's what happened in 1942 when Pepsi and Disney got together to produce matchbooks with military insignias on them. There were 48 different insignias in the complete set. Each matchbook is numbered.

DISNEY MATCHBOOKS

1942	Set of 48	D	$250
Individual	Matchbook	C+	$3 each

STRAWS

1940   D- $350
12" tall

1939   E $600
11" tall

1943   E $350
10" tall

STRAWS

1940   D $500
11" tall

1940   D $500
11" tall

1940   D $500
11" tall

STRAWS

| 1943 | C+ | $200 | 1945 | D | $350 |
| 10" tall | | | 11" tall | | |

| 1951 | D+ | $300 | 1954 | C+ | $150 |
| 11" tall | | | 11" tall | | |

TOYS

◄
1951   C+ $15
        Paper

1960   C $10
    Heavy Paper ►

TOYS

1940   D+ $100
Magic Pad

▸

◂

1965   C- $5
Heavy Paper

TOYS

▲ 1950   D $100
Miniature Billboard

▲ 1960   C $25
Miniature

TOYS

▲ 1980   B $10
Miniature Billboard

▲ 1940   C+ $50
Whistle

TOYS

◄ 1976   B $35
26" tall

1976   C $50 ►
Battery Operated
26" tall

TOYS

1963   B $10
Yo-Yo

1960   B $10
Yo-Yo

TOYS

1988   A $2
Yo-Yo

◄

►
1965   B $10
Yo-Yo

TOYS

1970   A $3
        Ball   ▶

▲ 1964   C $15
    Golf Balls

TOYS

1940   D $45
Game

1940   D+ $50
Game

TOYS

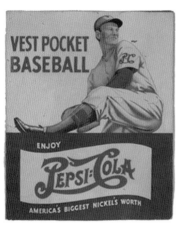

▲ 1940   C+ $100
Game

1980   B   ► $15
Baseball Bat

TOYS

▲ 1951   C+ $25

Board Game

◄

1951   C+ $25

Bingo Card

TOYS

1969   B $10
Paper Kite

1960   C+ $150
Miss America Doll

TOYS

1960   C+ $125
Playset

1980   B $45
Musical Dolls

TOYS

1970   A   ▲ $5

Toy Dispenser

1960   B+ $35

Toy Dispenser

TOYS

1995   B   ▲ $15

24" Inflatable

◄

1965   C $45

6' Inflatable

TOYS

▲ 1960   C $20
12" Inflatable

1988   A $5
12" Inflatable

▶

TOYS

▲ 1940   D $500
Pull Toy

◀

1956   D $225
Battery Operated

TOYS

◄ 1945   D $200
Plastic

1940   C+ $125 ►
Bank

TOYS

1960   D+ $600
Bank

1940   D $250
Bank

TOYS

1960   B $25
        Bank

◄

1973   B $10
        Bank

►

TOYS

1943   D+ ▲ $800
Buddy L
Composition 24"

▲ 1950   D+ $500
Plastic 8"

TOYS

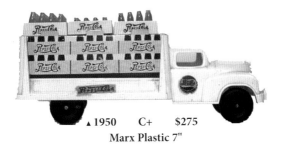

▲1950   C+ $275

Marx Plastic 7"

▲1940   C+ $125

Metal 6"

TOYS

▲ 1950   D $175
Tin Friction 7"

▲ 1954   D $150
Metal 6"

TOYS

▲ 1940   D+ $125
Metal 4"

▲ 1945   D $175
Tin Friction 5"

TOYS

▲ 1954   D $450
Cragsten Metal 11"

▲ 1951   D $275
Metal Friction 9"

TOYS

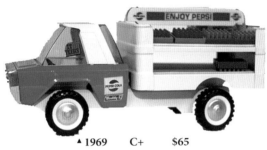

▲ 1969   C+ $65
Buddy L Metal 15"

▲ 1960   C+ $45
Metal 4"

TOYS

▲ 1980   B $10

Matchbox 6"

▲ 1978   B $20

Buddy L Set 10"

TOYS

▲ 1980   A $10
Majorette 10"

▲ 1978   B- $10
Tootsie 6.5"

TOYS

1990   A $10
4"

▲ 1978   D $20
Metal 3"

TOYS

▲1978   B $10
          3"

▲1990   A $10
          4"

TIP TRAYS

1908   E+ $3,800

6"

TIP TRAYS

Tip trays are also known as change trays. When a soda fountain patron was presented with a bill, it came on one of these trays. When the bill was paid, the change was placed on these trays. The early trays are very popular with collectors, causing the prices to continually increase.

TIP TRAYS

1909   D $1,200

◄   6"

1910   D $1,200

         6"

TIP TRAYS

1906   E $1,500

6"

TRAYS

Trays are one of the oldest and most consistently used promotional items in the soft drink industry. Early Pepsi trays are among the most sought after collectibles by collectors of Pepsi and advertising memorabilia. Due to their popularity, the prices of the early trays are constantly increasing.

1939   D $650
14" x 11"

TRAYS

1909   D+ $1,800
        14"   ▶

◀
1908   E $4,000
        14"

TRAYS

1939   D+ $750
12" dia.

1940   C+ $75
14" x 11"

TRAYS

1940   A $20 ▲
  14" x 11"   1940   A $20
                                  14" x 11"
                                      ◀

TRAYS

◄

1950   C+ $250
10" x 14"

1987   A $20
14" x 12"
New Haven, MO

▶

TRAYS

1967   B $15

    12" x 12"

1976   A $10

    14" dia.

VENDOR CAPS

▲1940   D $85
Cloth

▲1958   B $15
Paper

▲1963   B $10
Paper

MISCELLANEOUS

| 1940 | D | ▲ | $45 | 1960 | C | ▲ | $15 |
| Necktie | | | | Necktie | | | |

MISCELLANEOUS

1940   E   ▲ $250
Apron

1970   A   ▲ $5
Necktie

MISCELLANEOUS

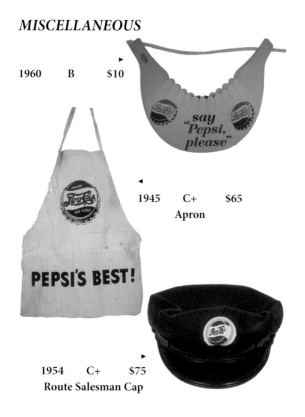

1960   B $10

say "Pepsi, please"

1945   C+ $65
Apron

1954   C+ $75
Route Salesman Cap

MISCELLANEOUS

1960   D $35
Plastic

1954   C+ $10
Felt Hat

MISCELLANEOUS

1960   C+ $75
Trash Can

1954   D $150
Toy Pepsi Stand

MISCELLANEOUS

▲ 1940   E $150
Flag

1964   C+ $150
Umbrella   ▶

MISCELLANEOUS

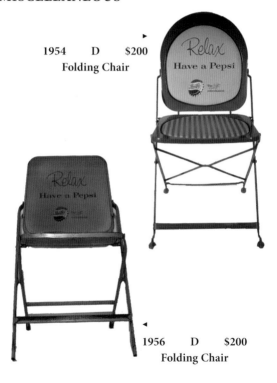

1954   D $200
Folding Chair

1956   D $200
Folding Chair

MISCELLANEOUS

1951   E+ $3,000
Scale ◄

1954   D+ $150
Teepee ►

MISCELLANEOUS

1951   C+ $90
    Whistle

1951   D $250
    Umbrella

MISCELLANEOUS

1975   C $35

Golf Bag

1978   B $30

Cake Tin

PAPER

All companies generate volumes of printed material. The Pepsi-Cola Company is no exception. Over the last one hundred years, the Pepsi-Cola Company, its bottlers, suppliers, and other affiliated companies have created millions of paper items. This includes documents, letters, brochures, internal publications, and other paper items needed to run a company that sells consumer products.

Included in this section is everything from coupons to postcards, from historically important documents to everyday advertisements. To many, these paper items may seem the least important of Pepsi collectibles, but the opposite is true. The documents, advertising books, brochures, and other paper items of the Pepsi-Cola Company are invaluable in determining what and when Pepsi items were produced. Beyond that, these items have helped with identification, dating, and understanding when and why trademarks have changed. It is because of the items in this section that we know as much as we do about the memorabilia of the Pepsi-Cola Company.

Besides the usefulness of these items, there is intrinsic value in owning letters and other documents created by the entrepreneurs who built the Pepsi-Cola Company. There is no other part of Pepsi-Cola collecting that is as exciting as finding old documents that shed new light on the history and the memorabilia of the Pepsi-Cola Company.

BLOTTERS

▲ 1905　　D　　$175

▲ 1905　　E　　$250

10" x 4"

▲ 1929　　D　　$200

7" x 4"

BLOTTERS

▲ 1940   C+ $125
7" x 4"

▲ 1943   D $175
7" x 4"

▲ 1945   C $75

BOOKLETS

▲ 1917   C+ $45
Notebook/Calendar

▲ 1939   D- $35
Notebook/Calendar

BOOKLETS

Booklets like these were given out to Pepsi consumers as early as 1914. Tens of thousands were distributed, but only a relatively small quantity survived.

BOOKLETS

1940 ▲ D- $35
Show Program

1941 ▲ C+ $35
Guide

▲ Reverse of above right

BOOKS

◄
1940　E　$350
Promotional Book

1956　D　$225
Promotional Book ►

BOOKS

▲ 1952   D $225
Promotional Book

▲ 1953   D $225
Promotional Book

BOOKS

◄

1969   C+ $75
Promotional Book

1963   B $25
▼ Promotional Book

BOOKS

1987　　B　　$25
Promotional Book

1951　　C+　　$15
Sales Training Book

BOOKS

◄ 1956   B+ $5
Sales Training
Booklet

► 1936   E $200
Promotional Booklet

BOOKS

1938   D $200
Anniversary Booklet
▶

◀
1940   E $200
Promotional Booklet

BROCHURES

▲ 1936   E $300
36" x 24" Brochure

▲ 1950   D $75
Promo Banner
22" x 34"

BROCHURES

▲ 1940   D $75

Brochure

▲ 1950   D $75

Promo Banner
22" x 34"

BROCHURES

◄

1940   C+ $35
Contest Sheet
8.5" x 11"

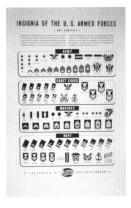

►

1944   D $35
Promo Flyer
8.5" x 11"

BROCHURES

1936   D $125
Brochure

1945   C+ $25
Brochure

BROCHURES

◄ 1949   D $85
Brochure

▶
1945   D $150
Advertising Booklet

BROCHURES

1940   D $50
Brochure

1946   C+ $25
Brochure

BROCHURES

◄ 1960   C+ $25
Brochure

1951   D $65
Brochure

BROCHURES

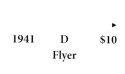

1941   D $10

Flyer

◄ **1943   D $10**

Flyer

BROCHURES

◄

1949   D $10
Flyer

►

1940   D $50
Flyer

BROCHURES

► 1936   D $50
Flyer

◄ 1939   D $10
Flyer

BROCHURES

1951   D $10

Flyer

1940   D $40

Flyer

COUPONS

▲ 1905   E $275

▲ 1905   E $275

COUPONS

▲1910   D $65

1940   D $50   ▶

▲1940   D $25

ENVELOPES

▲ 1917   E $50

Letter

▲ 1931   E $25

Letter

ENVELOPES

▲ 1939   C+ $25
Legal

▲ 1940   D $20
Legal

▲ 1941   C+ $15
Legal

ENVELOPES

▲ 1943　　C+　　$15

Letter

▲ 1940　　B　　$10

Check

▲ 1940　　A　　$5

Check

MAILERS

◄

1917   E $250
Advertising Mailer

1938   D+ $35
▼   Mailer

This is a very rare advertising mailer sent out by the Pepsi-Cola bottler, soliciting home sales of Pepsi-Cola. This would make a spectacular addition to any collection.

MAILERS

▲ 1940　　D+　　$125

Mailer

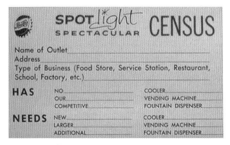

▲ 1960　　B　　$5

Mailer

MAILERS

▲ 1958   C $5
Mailer

▲ 1957   C+ $5
Mailer

GREETING CARDS

1960   C $10

1960   C+ $15

GREETING CARDS

1960   ▲ B $5

1972   C   ▶ $10

GREETING CARDS

1991 ▲ A $2

◄

1980   B $5
Wrapping Paper

LETTERHEAD

1917   E $500

Bradham

1915   E $200

1931   E $200

1930   D+ $100

LETTERHEAD

1939   C+ $15

1941   D $50

Mack

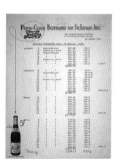

1940   C $10

1950   C $10

COLLECTING NEWSPAPER ADS

The best way to collect old Pepsi-Cola ads is to go to the library, and research the old newspapers. Once you have located the dates that the Pepsi ads appeared in, you can contact a dealer of old newspapers and order the dates you need.

1907   D $45

COLLECTING NEWSPAPER ADS

1908 ▲ D $45

PEPSI=COLA.

(The Pepsin Drink)

The most delightfully refreshing drink at Soda Fountains, helps digestion; cures headache and that "tired feeling." Try it for your "stomache sake."

5 Cents.
BRADHAM'S FOUNTAIN.

1908 ▲ D $35

◄

1902   D+ $20

Drop In Ad

COLLECTING NEWSPAPER ADS

1917 ▲ D $45

1917 ▲ D $45

1919 ► D $45

COLLECTING NEWSPAPER ADS

and happiness, refreshment and delight, all
packed together in one wonderful drink—

FOUNDED 1896

THE NATIONAL PEPSI-COLA CORP.
1224 West Broad Street
Richmond, Va.

▲ 1929   D $25

Presenting to Baltimore--the

BIG, NEW
12-OUNCE
Bottle of Delicious

        1934   D $25

COLLECTING NEWSPAPER ADS

1937 ▲ E $250   1936 ▲ C $10

▲1947 C+ $20

MAGAZINE ADS

1939   D $30

1941   C $15

MAGAZINE ADS

▲ 1940   C $15

▲ 1940   C $15

MAGAZINE ADS

▲ 1940   C $5

▲ 1942   C $5

MAGAZINE ADS

▲ 1942   C+ $15

▲ 1941   C $5

MAGAZINE ADS

▲ 1945   C $5

◄
1940   C $10

MAGAZINE ADS

▲1945   B $5

1943   A   ► $3

MAGAZINE ADS

▲ 1944 A $5

◄ 1943 C $10

MAGAZINE ADS

▲1947   C $10

1947   B $5 ▶

MAGAZINE ADS

1947   B $5 ▶

◀ 1951   B $5

MAGAZINE ADS

◄

1952   **B**   **$3**

►

1954   **A**   **$2**

MAGAZINE ADS

1960   A $2 ▶

◀

1960   B $5

MAGAZINE ADS

◄ 1959   A $2

► 1961   A $2

MAGAZINE ADS

1964   A $2

1967   A $2

MAGAZINE ADS

◄

1969   A $2

►

1970   B $5

MENUS

1950   C+ $25

1943   C $100

MENUS

◄ 1951   C+ $20

1962   C+ $15 ►

PEPSI PUBLICATIONS

1940 E $100 ▶

◀ 1940 E $100

PEPSI PUBLICATIONS

◄

1941   D $40

►

1945   D $40

PEPSI PUBLICATIONS

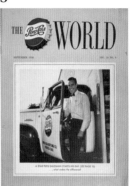

1956   C $20

◄

1958   B $5

PEPSI PUBLICATIONS

◄ 1969   A $3

► 1980   A $2

PEPSI PUBLICATIONS

▲ 1955   D $40
Annual Report

▲ 1958   D $40
Pepsi History
Brochure

PEPSI PUBLICATIONS

◄
1959   C+ $25
Annual Report

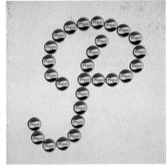

1962   C+ $15
Pepsi History
Brochure
►

MISCELLANEOUS

1973   C+ $20
Anniversary
Promotion

1941   C $25
Program

MISCELLANEOUS

▲ 1950   C+ $50

▲ 1950   C+ $50

MISCELLANEOUS

▲ 1950   C+ $50

▲ 1964   C+ $5
Book Cover

MISCELLANEOUS

1940   ▲ C $15
Bingo Token

1977   B $1
Trading Card

▶

1950   C+ $15
Golf Score Card ▼

MISCELLANEOUS

1963   B $5

Pageant Souvenir

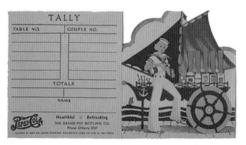

▲1940   C+ $65

Bridge Score Sheet

MISCELLANEOUS

◄

1940   C $75

Bridge Pad

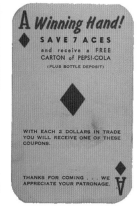

1960   C $2   ►

Game Piece

MISCELLANEOUS

1940 ▲ D+ $200
**Bottle Hanger/
Booklet**

1940 ▲ D+ $150
Bottle Hanger

1945 ▲ D $70
Bookmark

MISCELLANEOUS

1940   D+ $50
◄   Booklet

1945 ▲ D $70
Bookmark

◄
1960   D $10
Table Menu

MISCELLANEOUS

1960   C $5
Bottle Hanger

1956   C+ $5
Carton Stuffer

MISCELLANEOUS

1960   C $10 ▲
    Coaster

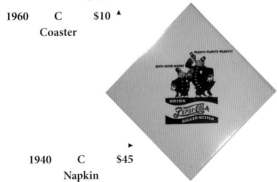

1940   C   ► $45
    Napkin

MISCELLANEOUS

▲1944   C $45
Stock Certificate

▲1945   C $45
Stock Certificate